S0-DJY-805

Chi, Feng Shui & You

How to Empower your
Life and Home with
Harmonious, Healthy and
Prosperous Feng Shui Energy!

by Kathy Mann

Published by Abundant Feng Shui Creations
PO Box 20683, Tampa, FL 33622,
www.fengshui108.com
888-339-9927

Copyright © 2007. All rights reserved. No part of this book may be reproduced or transmitted in any form or by any means, electronic or mechanical, including photocopying, recording, any digital means – email, text message, blogs, newsletters, etc., or by any information storage and retrieval system without written permission from the author, except for the inclusion of brief quotations in a review.

Dedication

To You.

To the seeker of healing energy, peace, love, health, knowledge and wealth.

May the energy of His Holiness Grandmaster Lin Yun's teaching touch your heart and soul, while empowering your life in the most suitable way for your highest good, right now.

May the peace, harmony, and all higher energy we seek begin inside each of us (our interiors) and RADIATE outside each of us (exteriors).

Let us all Shine!

Acknowledgements

My everlasting gratitude and joy can barely be expressed in this medium. Thank You, Xie Xie and Namaste!

To the overwhelming positive energy of Feng Shui that I felt and connected with when I discovered Feng Shui, it has opened up my life and doors in ways that would have never been possible without it.

To my parents and grandparents who have influenced my life in so many ways.

To my educational teachers in grammar school through college that encouraged me to love to learn.

To all my spiritual teachers and guides that helped me along my path of empowerment since January 1986. I would not be anywhere without you. The road has been a continuous adventure.

To all my Feng Shui teachers – there have been many Katrine Karley, Seann Xenja, Melanie Lewandowski, Katherine Metz, —— all of the teachers in the Feng Shui Conferences from 1996 to 2001 that were open to all Styles of Feng Shui —— Denise Linn, Karen Kingston, Steven Post, Barry Gordon, Edgar Sung, Juan Alvarez, David Kennedy, William Spear, Terrah Collins, Lillian Garnier, Nancy Santopietro, Dennis Fairchild, Catherine Woo, Ho Lynn, Jes Lim, …etc

Most especially to His Holiness Grandmaster Lin Yun and Crystal Chu Rinpoche for the dozens and dozens of weekend workshops, special engagements, retreats, field trips, yearly calendars, trips to Taiwan, coming to Tampa in 2003, that I have had been fortunate to experience.

To all the volunteers and helpers at the Temple who make all the functions work; Frances Li, Robert Chiu, Sheena, Patty, Greta, Chris, Shellie, Betty, these are only a few of the many contributors who make Feng Shui easily accessible for all of us. (Thanks to Dr Lien in Boston for hosting the Harvard class now for 13 plus years!)

佛

觀者順　念者安　得壽福存者壽

雲林禪寺　寺禪　雲　持無量咒

祈福

About the Author

Kathy Mann discovered Feng Shui while on a spiritual retreat, its purpose was to r e-connect, re-balance and grow spiritually. She was not looking for a career or unique life purpose. This is how it happened. This is her story.

When I saw Sara Rossbach's book – 'Interior Design with Feng Shui', it was an instant connection. I was born and raised in New Jersey, an Irish Italian Catholic, so an Asian spiritual and mystical concept of harmony for the home, empowering the person was never on my mind. I began a healing journey encompassing the mind, body and spirit January 1986. I have enjoyed exploring and utilizing metaphysical spirituality and many other avenues of positive personal growth.

As funny as it may sound, I know that Feng Shui is something that I was meant to do. It came to me, at the most auspicious time. I love helping people, love houses-homes, business-office buildings and environments in general."

In the early 90's there were not many books on Feng Shui. I bought all I could. I asked people who owned Chinese restaurants where I could learn more, and the reactions were sometimes comical. There was a consultant in Sarasota Florida who I employed to Feng Shui my house. Through miscommunication, what she said the fee was for the consultation was actually per hour, I do not think I would have hired her simply due to the cost, feeling it was a luxury. God has a way of directing the chi so that we are open to what is best for us. After the consultant left, I ran to Pier One, bought a few mirrors. Then I went to Publix for garbage bags, to pile up my excess clutter, especially clothing. That night I cleared clutter and moved all the furniture I could on my own. A friend came over in the morning and helped me move my bed. I exclaimed without thinking "I am going to do this for a living" My life began to change at that moment, many miracles have happened along the way. I have met incredible people from all walks of life, that I would have missed had I stayed in a cubicle, doing safe work.

Within a couple of months, I started to fly around the country taking weekend and week long classes. I practiced on friends houses. Within a year, my love for Feng Shui grew to a point where I wanted to do it more. In Florida, it was not well accepted at the time, yet my corporate work was unrewarding however the salary was adequate. I did a special method to help me decide and get clarity. I would wake every morning and use the sacred sun moon mirror. One day, I looked on my dresser and noticed a small photo of my father. He passed away very young in 1988. As a child he wasn't around much, yet in the last years of his life, he gave so much to others and lived a very spiritual life. It was a wonderful transformation to see. At the time of his passing, I asked his closest friends for a photo of him. I choose the one I liked the most, cut everyone else out, and framed it in a 2" by 3" frame. It was this photo I saw that morning. It hit me like a thunder bolt. Behind him on the wall was a Chinese calligraphy. I found someone to translate for me. I cried upon hearing that it meant LOVE. When I was 16 and my Dad was fresh out of rehab, he gave me the only real advice he said " Kath, do what you love, do not harm anyone and you will be happy." I loved Feng Shui. So, in the next 18 months, I began building a business, continued my Feng Shui education, then finally began Feng Shui full time. It has not been easy, and I am not wealthy, but when people tell me of the positive shifts in their lives, the goals they achieved ease, the house selling after being on the market a long time, to awareness they were resisting, to health being helped, wealth enhanced, relationships created or healed, and so much more. It fills my heart and soul like nothing else can.

I still wonder how I got here.

Many times I have leaped without the mundane thoughts of how can I get there. Not everyone I love or loves me understands why I need to do this work, and I have lost some dear friends. My family tolerates it and some think I will grow out of it. My life changed when I applied Feng Shui to my home and it continues to be empowered. Many miracles have happened along the way. I speak at corporate programs, teach wherever there is interest, and lecture for many organizations and women's groups. By my nature, I am shy, yet when I begin to share on Feng Shui an energy and confidence takes over that allows me to be in my authentic power to help people on many levels. Sometimes, if someone changes one thing in their home, their lives are enhanced each day which has incalculatable benefits. I am still in awe of these results. The information I give to people are the mystical teachings of HH Grandmaster Lin Yun, yet the people are the ones who really make the changes in their lives.

I have met incredible people from all walks of life, I learn from each person and the goodness that lies in each one of us. My clients are open and really have the trust and faith that this work is special. All of this I would have missed had I stayed in a cubicle, doing safe work, being normal in the eyes of most of the world However, it is normal for me to know that your environment affects you, and it is simple common sense to make sure that it is making a positive impact on your life in all aspects. I love what I do.

For a full description of my credentials doing Feng Shui see pages 150-153.

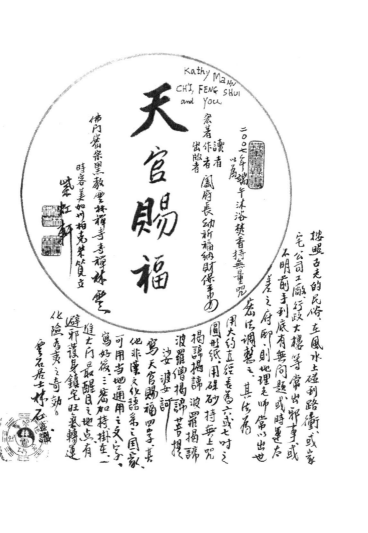

Top calligraphy, inscription from right:

Written with cinnabar after offering incense and chanting infinite numbers of mantras, on the Dragon Boat Festival, the Fifth Day of the Fifth Lunar Month, 2007.This calligraphy bestows Blessings upon the entire households to the author, publisher, and readers of this masterpiece, and prays that they receive auspicious luck, increased wealth and safety.

Center calligraphy:Heavenly Magistrates Bestow Blessings

Composed by Grandmaster Lin Yun of Black Sect Tantric Buddhism Yun Lin Temple, while a visitor at the Berkeley, California study of disciple Crystal Chu.

Bottom inscriptions, from right:

According to ancient folklore, if one's Feng Shui arrangement is that the road leads straight on towards one's house; or if bad or abnormal events often take place at one's residence, office building, or factory; of if one is not clear about the situation with one's predecessors; or if one just constantly runs into bad luck, then geomancy advisors often prescribe transcendental solutions to adjust one's Feng Shui.One of these methods is to take a round-shaped piece of paper with a diameter of six or seven inches, and while chanting the Heart Calming Mantra (Gate gate, para gate, para sum gate, bodhi swaha), write with cinnabar the four characters, "Heavenly Magistrates Bestow Blessings."Those people from countries not using Chinese characters could use their own languages to translate these four characters.After it is written, while using the Three Secret Reinforcements, hang the piece of round paper at the most conspicuous and easily seen place upon entering one's front door.This transcendental solution has the amazing effect of warding off evil, offering protection to one's person and residence, turning one's Ch'i and luck from bad to good, and evading any danger that might take place.

Lin Shr*

*Lin Shr is one of the many scholarly names of His Holiness Grandmaster Professor Lin Yun.

風水自然和諧最好

虎雲龍假亦真
清樹茂見精神
由自在充天地
否否然格物新
戰平分全世界
莊佈滿大乾坤
是緣生緣滅處
將大道告知音

觀者順念者安得者福存者壽
二〇〇七年端午碟書持咒以為
大著讀者作者編者盧府
祈福增慧

Kathy Mann
CH'I, FENG SHUI
and You

風水

佛門密宗黑教林雲禪院
院禪林
雲書於覽紫虹軒
立仁波切柏克萊

Top, "Hidden Title Poem" from right

Tiger appears in wind,
Dragon arrives in clouds,
This seems so unreal, yet also so true.
Water is crystal-clear,
Trees are lush and green,
All things are high-spirited,
As comfort and ease
Pervade the entire universe
Be it yes or no, right or wrong,
Only after thorough learning
Will new knowledge be acquired.
Peace and warfare have always been
Prevalent throughout the world,
Just as jest and dignity happen
Everywhere between heaven and earth.
The ultimate is to understand
That karma begins and ceases,
And to share this great knowledge
With confidants who care to know.

Bottom inscription, from right:

"To see these words will bring you smooth luck
To recite these words will bring you peace
To receive these words will bring you prosperity
To preserve these words will bring you longevity."

Written with cinnabar on the Dragon Boat Festival, the Fifth Day of the Fifth Lunar Month, 2007, to bestow blessings upon the entire households of the author, editor and readers of this great book, and pray that they receive auspicious luck and increased wisdom.

Center Calligraphy, from the top: FENG SHUI

Written by Lin Yun of Black Sect Tantric Buddhism Lin Yun Monastery, while a visitor at the study of disciple Crystal Chu.

Table of Contents

Appendix I

A complete list of detailed, and advanced teachings

Appendix II

Appendix III

"CH'I, FENG SHUI and YOU"
PREFACE
By
His Holiness Thomas Yun Lin Hon. Ph.D.
Abbot Grandmaster, Fourth Stage Black
Sect Tantric Buddhism

I am extremely pleased to be the first one to see the original draft of Kathy Mann's book *Ch'i, Feng Shui and You.* I have studied Feng Shui for more than 60 years; I have taught, analyzed and practiced Feng Shui for at least 62 years or more.

My students and disciples can be divided into three types.

1. The first kind, the "wisdom" type, who after I teach them just one corner, can draw the entire square or after hearing one piece of information, can think of 10 other items of knowledge. Sometimes, they are even able to discover some secret-within-secret's that I haven't taught them.

2. This second type, the "pragmatic" type, do not cause others to think of them as being the most brilliant of people. Yet they also have their own wisdom. However, their method of studying is that they do not miss a single word of what I say or write and very clearly remember every picture I draw. When they are helping others analyze or adjust their Feng Shui, the mundane, transcendental or secret-within-secret methods they use are all completely true to my teachings.

3. The third type of students are those who only know to pay their tuition but they don't listen, take any notes, or make any sound or video recordings, yet they attend every class no matter where the classes are held. I like the third type of students best, because they come to class purely to sup-

port me and be loyal to me; they love me more than any other people love me. Since they don't listen, they don't even know how to ask any questions. When others ask questions, they feel the questions are strange and they think the people asking these questions are even stranger.

But the author of this book, Kathy Mann, is not of the last type, my favorite. Of course, I believe that she should belong to the first "wisdom" type of disciples because she also hears one thing and knows 10 other things and learns one corner and can draw the other three corners of the square. Because she especially respects my lectures' original meaning and teachings of the transcendental solutions' original cures and original mantras, therefore, the impression that she gives to others is that she is a role model of the "pragmatic" type. Perhaps, she also gives people this impression because she is cultured, refined, humble, polite, serene and reticent.

The contents of the book *Ch'i, Feng Shui and You* are quite broad, covering what is Feng Shui, the basic fundamental principles of Feng Shui, the Feng Shui of Ba Gua (Eight Triagrams) and the applications of Ba Gua in Feng Shui, the content of basic mundane and transcendental cures, and the meaning of the Three Secret Reinforcements.

Moreover, the book explains why Feng Shui Practitioners must receive red envelopes from their clients, just as medical doctors and lawyers receive fees for their services, and why in the interior design of a house – the various concepts such as the design of the bed, the stove, the desk and the main door are based on their "relative" positions rather than "absolute" directions.

The author also notes many mundane facets, the details to which architects should pay attention; also the type of interior design which includes consideration of the Ba Gua (Eight Triagrams), the five elements, the theory of Yin Yang (The Tao of I Ching) and its secret meaning (the meaning of

Tantric Buddhism's spiritual contents).

Also, other than factors which we can see: such as the Ch'i of the Land, the shape of the lot, the internal structure of the house (master bedroom, kitchen, and position of the main door and the Feng Shui design), and "other" factors, such as the internal factors (beams, stairs, placement of the bed, the positioning of the office desk, study desk, and dining table, where should the stove be put, whether the main door should open to the left or right, the relative positions of the doors of the different rooms, the brightness or dimness of lights, the choice of colors, the entrance of the cold air from the air conditioner ... and sky lights) are one of the classes of factors that must be considered in interior design.

Also there are the "external" factors, such as the environment outside of the buildings, residences, the yard, and the factory. For example, are there roads directly running in the direction of the house, is the front door blocked by big trees? Are there bridges, rivers or intersecting roads, airports, funeral homes, telephone poles (or power lines)? Or is the house in front of temples or behind churches or trash burners, public cemeteries or nuclear waste storage areas; also gates to the country by land, boundaries with neighboring countries, gates to the country in the air (airports), gates to the country from the ocean (ports), etc.

Other than these, the author also discusses factors that physical eyes cannot see but especially emphasized by Black Sect Tantric Buddhism, i.e. intangible factors, including the Three Secret Reinforcements, the Nine-Star Path, the determination of the Ba Gua (Eight Triagrams), the Constant Turning Dharma Wheel, Internal Ch'i Adjustment, External Ch'i Adjustment, the Predecessor Factor; other considerations related to blessings, ground breaking, driving away evil influences, transcendence, getting auspiciousness, accumulating wealth, communicating with spirits, praying to deities in fortune telling, chanting sutras and mantras, and other special ceremonies.

The reader, after reading this book, will discover that the author has applied traditional Feng Shui principles to today's life, being compatible with scientific knowledge to allow people living on earth to become acclimated with nature, and overcome flawed environments to obtain the most comfortable conditions for life.

So, whether your profession is an industrialist, architect, environmentalist, landscape designer, Feng Shui practitioner, psychotherapist, whoever has this popular book and or reads it, will receive unimaginable benefits, what the Ancients call, "just opening the book brings benefits. Therefore I am delighted to write this preface and am even happier to recommend the author and her great work.

H.H. Lin Yun Thomas Hon. Ph.D.
Spring 2007
Abbot
Zen Master of Yun Lin Temple

Written in the study of Crystal Chu Rinpoche, CEO of Black Sect Tantric Buddhism;
Translated by Dr. George Lee, Professor of International Business and Director of US-Eurasia Institute of San Francisco State University

Chapter 1
Feng Shui is...

What is Feng Shui Really?

Feng Shui is how your environment affects you. In Feng Shui we wish to create the most suitable, comfortable, beautiful, functional and positive feeling space for the people who dwell in it. A home is more than a space that provides shelter. It is a nurturing private space that is compatible with you in every way possible. We look at the Feng Shui of a home on many levels with you in mind at all points.

It is all about creating the most energetically compatible space in which to live, work, and spend time! If we are in harmony with our spaces, it allows for a more fulfilling experience in all areas of our lives. It can support you to reach your highest potential. When the chi is in alignment with you and healthy for you in your home, you won't deplete your energy/chi in achieving your goals in life. When your chi/energy is high, you can more easily achieve goals and overcome obstacles. It is also said that when your chi is high, it does not attract negativity or misfortune. This does not mean that nothing 'negative' will ever happen when you do your Feng Shui well, however you will gain an advantage and life is smoother.

Using most aspects of Feng Shui is very logical, it makes sense, common sense. Taoists began Feng Shui study and application. They realized the importance of living in balance with nature. The gifts of nature were to be cherished and used with respect and appreciation, not to conquer or destroy but to co-habitat harmoniously. They found harmony led to prosperity in all aspects of life.

And Feng Shui, well, Black Sect Feng Shui as taught by H.H. Grandmaster Lin Yun, can be much more. It can help you to transform your life. In conjunction with the mundane factors of a good life, living consciously and by honorable spiritual principles, doing mundane tasks, raising your chi in regard to your mind, body and spirit along with Feng Shui, wonderful things occur frequently. Plus when obstacles occur, you can overcome them more quickly and smoothly.

In this style of Feng Shui there are numerous levels of the energy work that can be recommended. It is not always on the visible level. It is rich in ancient wisdom that covers many different types of healing and energy shifting. In this book, we will cover the basics, plus a few of the various other higher realms of energy shifting. If you need more recommendations for a given situation or illness, let us know and we will let you how that can be accomplished.

Before we get into the how to, please know and understand that not all schools of Feng Shui are alike. These schools/approaches or styles do not always blend well together. They are all wonderful and effective. A good way to describe the differences may be like different languages, different interior design styles, different cooking styles, and different psychology methods and so on. They all work, sometimes a blend may work, sometimes it may feel, sound, taste or look funny together. This book will only address working with Black Sect Feng Shui as HH Grandmaster Lin Yun has taught.

It was recommended to me, in the beginning days of my study of Feng Shui, to avoid confusion, to only learn one style at a time. At that time, there were a little more than a handful of books on the market. Now there are hundreds of books on the market. When choosing a book, it helps to know that the author has studied extensively with a Master. A list of the authentic Black Sect Books is in the appendix of this book. Even though, I have done some study with masters in other styles of Feng Shui, my choice was to go into deeper study with His Holiness Grandmaster Lin Yun and not to mix and match or to learn a lot of schools on a surface level. Trust your intuition and study what approach(es) you feel inspired to learn.

The reason for the different styles is quite simple. Through the thousands of years Feng Shui has been used and studied, needs and information available at that time and place were different. Influences were different. Cultures were different. The foundational principles that direct and influence each school may focus in a different area. In the form school, mostly visible influences will influence the how to of applying its principles. In some compass approaches, an astrological influence determines the direction, and the male head of household needs to have a positive chi flow first and foremost. Some schools are mostly or only concerned with balancing the five elements. There are numerous styles of Feng Shui. A number of new approaches have been created since Feng Shui came to the United States of America in the 1980's.

BTB Feng Shui, an affectionate nickname, is the school of Feng Shui which you will learn in this book. The official name is The Black Sect Tibetan Tantric Buddhism School of Feng Shui. Thus, BTB flows easily. In our approach, we want to take into consideration all information available to make our Feng Shui assessment. We acknowledge that environmental factors are different now and are constantly changing. Like the I-Ching, The Book of Changes, Feng Shui will evolve and change. It is natural to do so. We look at visible factors, invisible factors, study the chi from all senses, look at the chi of the land, chi of the structure, chi of the interior design, and chi of the people. The information we use combines modern knowledge and ancient wisdom. There are many influences in this style of Feng Shui; psychological, yin-yang philosophy, divination, holistic healing, Taoism, Folklore, Eclecticism, Mysticism, Confucianism, I-Ching, Tibetan Buddhism, Esoteric Buddhism, cultural imprints from India, Tibet and China, Five Element Energies, physiology, ecology, social sciences, knowledge of people and medicine. The approach is not narrow, but broad with many tools and focused on the precise needs of the person(s) in that place NOW. The process is to read the chi for the people and place in this moment, using all available knowledge to help the chi, people and Feng Shui.

The bottom line with Feng Shui is that your environment affects you. It does this subtly and directly. You have a conscious knowing of this and your subconscious is also influenced which you may or may not be aware of what you are feeling or what is influencing you most. You may have strong enough chi to overcome any negative energy in a space or otherwise. My thinking is why expend that energy to overcome, if you can be enhanced and uplifted by your home and work space. The more time you spend in any given space the more it has an affect on you. Spend time building your personal energy, so when you are visiting places with low energy you will not be affected.

Take advantage of Feng Shui and get an edge in life that can positively influence your health, wealth, family and relationships. Enjoy your home to the fullest potential. You may have heard of this quote by Winston Churchill. "First we shape our dwellings, then our dwellings shape us." You have the power and choice to shape your life, do it with accurate Feng Shui!

Use the principles in this book to make adjustments in your home. When and if you feel you have done all you can do, you may feel ready to have a consultant come out to your home. To search for a qualified consultant, takes a little effort. Go online to www.yunlintemple.org or ask friends or your acupuncturist or other holistic healers for a reference. Try the internet. When you do receive a name check their credentials. Ask about their study with a master or in a direct lineage with a Grandmaster or Master. Ask about length of study. At the present time there are no governing bodies or associations that have collaborated with all the authentic Grandmasters to create a uniform teaching program. Certification is a relative term. Ask about who created the certification and find out about that person's credentials. You can also check to be sure they are connected with the lineage to a Grandmaster or true Master. Becoming a true Master takes decades of full time work and study. Someone who takes a weekend class is not a Master, and is not thoroughly trained. I have seen people who feel they have a knack for it and barely read a book or take a two hour class and then proceed to start a business. Be careful. Ask for references.

Trust your intuition. With today's technological advances, many Feng Shui analyses can be done long distance. I do this all the time. Feng Shui consulting can be done in regards to selling houses-land and businesses, choosing floors plans, assessing fully decorated homes and businesses – to everything in between. If a chi adjustment is needed on your property, if your chi is in good shape and you may learn a method, or it may be best to bring someone to your area.

The definition of Feng Shui today is to create and maintain environments that will be completely supportive and uplifting to you and all who live and visit in your home. You can use Feng Shui as a tipping point to enhance your life in many ways, with visible methods, aesthetics, harmonizing chi and using the Bagua. Your environment affects you, direct it to be empowering and work for you, not against you.

Chapter 2
Energy & Foundation Principles

Chi —- The Heart of Feng Shui

Chi is energy. Everything has chi. We and all things are energetically connected in some way, form or fashion. Feng Shui harmonizes/aligns that connection. Your environment affects you by the energy that is created by you and all the things in and around it.

What is chi? It can be defined by many different variables. Therefore, the analysis of it is not fixed rigid or constant. States of energy are constantly changing as well. Intuitively we know a lot more than what we think. Each person is affected by energy differently. You may feel empowered more by water than anyone in your home. Another person may clearly feel the energies emitted from electrically powered objects or cell phones. Another aspect is that you may go through a period of time where any noise may wake you up, but the rest of life you would not be awoken by any noise. What we want to achieve with Feng Shui is to give you principles of energy as guidelines, then the specific assessment takes into account all factors of the exact place (hemisphere, country, town, neighborhood, road and building), specific time (now) and you as you are completely at this moment. We will also shift. Create Feng Shui to support all of your life's experiences.

Chi can be viewed from these points. Bear in mind the weight of each may differ in each space we assess.

The sense of yin and yang, day and night. male and female...etc.

What an item is made of – be it an interior décor object to the terrain of the land the building it is sited on has chi. Is it made of wood, metal, plastic, fabric... etc. Review the following list of how chi can be viewed.

- Color
- Placement or positioning
- The balance or imbalance of the 5 elements
- Symbolic meaning universally
- Symbolic meaning individually
- Symbolic meaning culturally
- Individual Taste
- Relevance to the room, or purpose in the space
- Importance
- Time quality – season, event, astrology
- Movement – type and quality thereof...
- Size
- Value
- Where it came from
- History (if any)
- A perception from all your senses
- Other... (we are evolving, more information is revealed to us all the time, plus we are inventing new things. These things may have a new energetic make-up, and/or when thrown into the current mix may make obvious or subtle changes to the chi and Feng Shui.

The overall chi of an item or space is a combination of all these factors and then some. Each factor may weigh differently in the given situation on that given day. From this basis, we are all not going to be enhanced by the same design in the same situation through all time.

Given this information, let's explore chi. Imagine that you walk into a room for an event. The walls are all beige. The curtains are drawn. There are no plants or art work. The seating is set up in a traditional classroom style. The floor is hardwood. The chairs are black. The room is 30 feet by 30 feet. Feel this energy by what I have described.

Now let's change the chi by doing one adjustment at a time. Imagine these changes and how it will feel different as the chi changes.

1. Take all of the information above and simply add 9 plants that are lush, lively and large. They are placed in balance around the room. Feel the difference.

2. Take all of the information above and change the color of the room to a warm medium shade of blue. It lifts your chi, it is pleasant and light.

3. Same room. Change the floor. Make it terrazzo. Then, try a commercial grade burgundy or hunter green carpet. Feel the color and texture change the energy.

4. Same room. Change the chairs make them gray. Next, try white.

5. Same room, change the lighting. Add more. Decrease lights.

6. Same room and change the position of the chairs. Use chairs that are more comfortable. Make them in a horseshoe shape. Add more chairs. Take some away. Add tables. If you see the back of the chairs as you enter, re-position so as you enter you see the seat of the chair. All of these changes will shift the chi in the room. The message is clear at the initial entry.

7. Same room. Now add three magnificent pieces of art. Add beautiful fresh flowers all around the room.

I can continually make up new rooms. The permutations are quite extensive. When you begin to design a room, begin with the purpose. How do you want the room to serve you? What do you need? How can you enhance the experience so everyone can get the most out of the experience.

What do you want to have the room say as people enter? What does the room need to convey as you are seated? Once you determine the purpose, needs, wants, and experience, you can design and place things to completely support that purpose. It is the same in a home. It is the same on the land of the home.

Chi is in everything and everyone. It flows throughout your space. It changes. You can direct it by how you allow the chi to be navigated around your space. We can create a distinctive energy. You can constantly add energy to keep the energy in your space high, positive and well balanced. Quality will be felt and experienced. Individual tastes will play a factor in every situation. Everything changes. The more time you spend in a place the more the effect can be. If the space, event or moment is very important, the energy will significantly influence you.

Professor has taught us that when your personal energy – chi – is high you can overcome anything. When your chi is low or weak, you are more susceptible to all the energy around you. He has often said we can live and be anywhere when our chi is high. Why let your space affect you negatively? Create a positive energetic experience. Do your Feng Shui, so that you can reach your potential with joy, harmony and not have it take your health or chi away. Let if flow.

Multiple Cause and Effect Theory

(HH Grandmaster Lin Yun's Theory)

Feng Shui can be used to change our luck, change our chi, change our karma, change our fate, change our destiny, and /or change our lives. Sounds simple! What makes our lives healthy, happy and successful in every way? Many things contribute to our success, health & happiness.

5 aspects of our life make our success and happiness
- Luck
- Fate/Destiny
- Feng Shui

- Education
- Accumulation of Good Deeds

No one action is the reason for any occurrence in our lives. If your chi is not ready to accept the good fortune, be it marriage, wealth or great health, you will not be able to create the outcome. Continued practice of chi cultivation; removing of past beliefs, processing of traumas and raising your energy with meditation, activities good for your mind, body and spirit with creating good karma through good deeds. You will shift the energy.

Feng Shui helps create the highest and best outcome for all concerned. So if it is not in your best interest it will not happen. When you do a cure to marry someone, and you realize it is not the best for you, the cure is a success. You will never make someone do something against their will. If the intended outcome is of the highest and best, it will happen.

An Analogy – Is anyone one of these things the only reason you did not get a cold this season? Vitamin C and/or other immune booster, washing your hands well especially in public places, good sleep habits, great nutrition, adequate exercise, drinking plenty of water, and avoiding people with colds or other infections. Not one of these can prevent a cold altogether. Feng Shui cannot work alone, nor is it the be all or end all. Bad Feng Shui can make your life's goals harder to attain! Feng Shui Cures, Adjustments and Enhancements can give an edge, can be a catalyst, prevent conflict, ease the flow, support your life's goals, unblock obstacles, create better moods, plus more, and make you feel good.

What makes Feng Shui work successfully?

Use Feng Shui with a Sincere Heart – Professor Lin Yun tells us this over and over, as it can be most important. An example of sincerity is simply doing your cures with a mindfulness and your heart energy, love.

Your Belief in it. The simple notion that it will work for you while you are still doing the mundane things to create the outcome. It gives you an edge or you know that the vibrations in your environment add to your existence. (if you have a member of your family that thinks what you are doing is silly, or will never work... etc; it may be best not to share the cures or do some of them in front of them.)

Timing (the highest and best job, house, partner, may not be ready or you are not) This aspect relates to astrology as well. Feng Shui can help bring awareness to issues, research or other information you need to work on or acquire.

Keeping it Special & Quiet at First - Not all cures, but many of the most transcendental & powerful ones, should be kept secret to your self and occupants of your home, especially until outcome is received. Once your goal is received, you may be inspired to help a family member or friend, but be sure to get red envelopes for the information.

No matter how much you love Feng Shui, do not tell people what to do with their homes, business structures without an invitation from them. Interfering like this affects the outcome of your success and theirs. Ask permission. Offer to help, then allow the desire to be from that person. Professor says, there needs to be a knock at the door, before you can answer. If the knock is soft, answer softly. When the knock is loud, give all you can to help. Honor the chi, honor your friends and family. You may offer a solution and if they are interested in the help, they can honor you with the red envelopes, setting up the energy for their success. Feng Shui is not for everyone, honor and respect that when someone is not interested.

The Front Door

The front door is known as the mouth of chi. It is how every-thing enters into the body of your house, the opportunities and energies that come into your life. It feeds all aspects of the house, all aspects of you. This statement is huge. It is how the chi that nourishes you comes to you. It is the beginning point of how chi enters, it can affect all parts of the Bagua, all aspects of your life. This is more symbolic, yet very powerful literally. It is very important.

In Black Sect Feng Shui, we overlay the Bagua beginning at the front door. This is done because it is how the chi enters. So, we are not concerned with which direction the door faces, but how you see it and can approach it from the road or walkway.

I look at the front door as being the piece of art, and the rest of the house frames it. I like it to be attractive, appealing, and to stand out beautifully. It should be more impressive than the garage. A red front door can be most appealing. Yet, if aesthetically it does not feel and look right, red may not work. A cherry red front door for instance, will usually not blend well with an orange Mediterranean style home. It should blend, yet pop out. The frame around the front door can be in several colors like the matting of a beautiful piece of art. If the house is a light color, the front door will be best if it is a medium to dark color shade. You will want to be practical as well. Here on the west coast of Florida, if you have a west facing door, the impact of the vibrant sun could mean extra maintenance or the fact that certain colors will simply not last with the colors vibrancy and appeal.

If you have a beautiful wood door that is carved and beautifully cared for, you probably will not wish or need to paint it. Make sure however if it is a dark shade of wood, that it is well framed by the house and that the dark shade does not make the entryway feel dark. I do come across many homes that are in deed restricted communities where only certain colors are allowed to be used. In these cases, we will usually add colorful flowers around or on the front door. There are a lot of different ways to embellish the front door so it stands out without it being a visible code violation in these restrictive living spaces. Adding beautiful embellishments around the front door should not be overdone. Anything around the front door should enhance its beauty and be inviting.

Clutter can occur outdoors as well as indoors. Make sure there is plenty of room to come and go from your home. Clutter can occur in your landscape. If the path to walk is four feet wide, yet you have plants that have overgrown into it, then you may possibly create limitation by allowing energy to come less to you. You do not want to have to do an obstacle course to enter and exit from your home.

A meandering pathway is the best design. If you have a straight path you can create a meandering feel by placing plants or landscape objects in this way. See below. You will feel the chi going from one special chi mover to the next thereby creating a meandering pathway on a yin level (invisible level). The feel is usually more important than the initial visual interpretation. If you place plants straight up and down a straight path you will accentuate the same rush of energy.

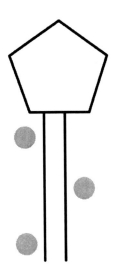

Create Meandering Path

Other factors that are important as it relates to the front door is how well defined your home is in regard to address number. If people have a hard time finding you with explicit directions, because the house numbers are off your mail box or muted so you can't see them on the house or the mailbox, it can create a poor flow of chi. You may miss opportunities in life and not fully enjoy all the areas of the Bagua. In this style of Feng Shui, the absolute direction is not of concern, yet seeing the front door from the road is very important. If you cannot see the door, the path to it should be very obvious and place adjusting cures outside the door to enhance the energy.

As you enter, first room seen...

The first room seen sets the tone for the energy in the home. Some rooms can have a negative impact while others will be inviting and can influence you and your family in a positive way. There is a real psychological component in this area. This area is very important when selling real estate. There is a lot more to selling real estate than this area, but it is a key area.

A bathroom first seen can be problematic for several reasons. You may think about elimination on the way home, even if you do not have to go to the bathroom. Upon arrival at home you may go to the bathroom immediately. When designing a home, avoid placing a bathroom at first sight from the front entry, and your most frequently used pathway upon entry, if you enter from the garage or a back door. Cures for an existing bathroom are to make sure that you cannot see it from the front door or place a crystal, wind chime or hanging plant in-between the door and the bathroom. Avoid seeing a bed upon entry. One may become lazy, sleep too much or have a pre-occupation with sex. Use the same methods to change the chi as with the bathroom.

Avoid seeing the stove. Your stove symbolizes health, wealth and career. All of those could be vulnerable if seen from the front door. Eating disorders may ensue. Money may be lost. A career may be in jeopardy. Overall struggles and disasters may occur. Use the same cures as above.

Avoid seeing a gambling table as first seen from the front door. The obvious may occur. Do the same cures.

Best rooms to see are a foyer, a den, a study or a living room. Most of all create a beautiful, open, well lit and inviting first impression. You can place books or objects you enjoy or want to spend more time doing. All your décor, art and over-all interior design will impact the energy in the home. It is a good idea to come into a well lit space. You can even install a light that will turn on when opening the door. Better yet, it can also activate beautiful sound. It will raise the chi of your home.

Exterior Chi

Where you live, the neighborhood has an influence on your chi. The actual land itself has chi defining factors. What surrounds you, the feeling, the five element connection, the history, reputation of communities, the flow and quality of land are a few ways to analyze the chi of the land.

The type of street you live on also has an impact. Cul-de-sac streets have one way in and one way out. Some gated com-munities have the same energy. The limiting chi can cause a stagnation of chi over time. It can contribute to clutter, confusion, struggles in any aspect of life. A weather vane on the roof is one way to keep the chi moving. There are several other ways to offset this chi. Many people like to live on cul-de-sac streets for minimal traffic flow and privacy. Do the cure so you can have your cake and eat it too. Dead end streets have a similar pattern of energy.

When someone lives at the end of a "T" street, it can create many different types of problems with chi. Like the shape of the T the road drives right up the house. We can use a Bagua mirror on the house or place a physical obstruction in-between the house and the street. This could be bushes, concrete walls, and large rocks or stones. On rare occasions a home is placed in a position where there is a double "T" street position. From the back and front of the home this sha chi is barreling toward the house. It needs adjustments on both the front and back.

Whenever there is something inauspicious in your neighborhood close to your house or directing its chi by architectural design of that house, an easy remedy is to place a Bagua mirror above your front door. This is a very powerful and ancient practice. It will stop the flow of that chi from coming inside the home. You could have an abandoned home, or a highway built near your home, or people living close who are suffering from a terminal or progressive illness, or nosey neighbors, transformer poles or boxes for the entire neighborhood, and much more. The convex mirror is also very effective. You may consider adding more vegetation between your home and the negative influence. Fruit and flowering plants, trees and bushes can be a most beneficial addition of chi to you and it helps the planet.

Chapter 3
The Bagua

Soul of Feng Shui Bagua

The Ever Changing Bagua is a major fundamental tool of Feng Shui. We can use this on a micro level and a macro level. The most important areas that you can overlay this map of energy are on your land, your home, your bedroom, and your bed. Your kitchen is another important space. Where you spend the most amount of time and any space that is significant to you are the best places to place the Bagua. A word of caution: it is not essential to place the Bagua over every single room in your home. It can cause overwhelm, (really wig you out) and it is ineffective in the grand scheme of things, in most situations. Less is more.

Here is the Bagua map.

Diagram #1: *The Bagua*

Wealth	Fame	Marriage/ Partnership
Family	Health	Children
Knowledge	Career	Helpful People & Friends

Mouth of Chi, how you enter, front door, driveway, room door...

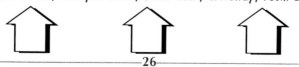

PLACING THE BAGUA ON YOUR LAND

Take the map and place the arrows on the entrance to your land, which in most cases is the driveway. If you have two driveways, it can either be the most frequently used entrance or the one that faces the street your address is on. If you do not have land, skip to the next section on placing the Bagua on your home. If the shape of your land is a rectangle, which many are, you can use a ruler over the land survey and choose inches or centimeters whichever is easier to divide by 3. Place little marks at the 1/3 then 2/3 spot. Next draw a line from the front to the back of the property at both of these points. Do this same procedure from side to side of the property. You now have a rectangular Bagua. You have created nine sections of your land.

It is recommended to draw a circle in each of your 9 rectangle boxes of the property. The reason for this is to see the softness of the transition from area to area. Feng Shui is not about hard rigid energy, it is about flow, smoothness of chi and balance.

Then I would write in the names of each area in each circle. When I have a small plot of land drawing, I will write in the letter of the area. The driveway will always be on the side that is named Knowledge/Spirituality, Career and Helpful People, Friends. You will not begin the Bagua from any other side of your Bagua map. The next section from left to right is family, health and children. The last one third areas are wealth, fame/reputation, and marriage/partnership/relationships.

Please review three different plots of land that have the Bagua traced on them. You can see how easy it is to do on a rectangular or square shaped piece of land.

Here are a few examples of the Bagua on a plot of land.

Diagram #2: *The Bagua on land*

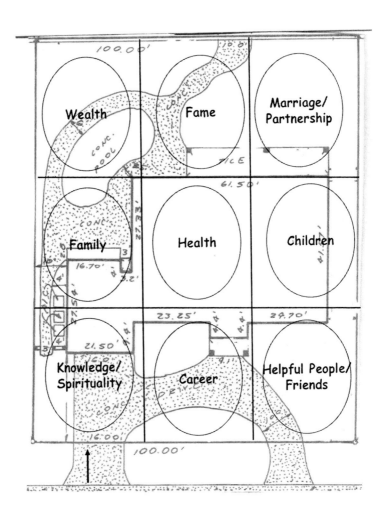

Diagram #3: *The Bagua on land*

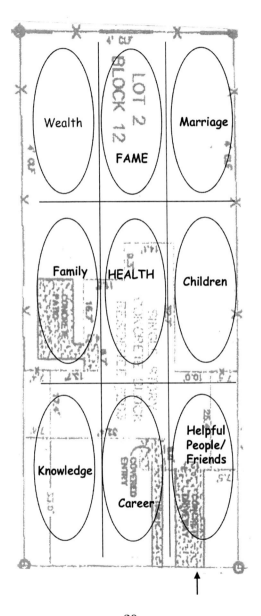

Diagram #4: *The Bagua on land*

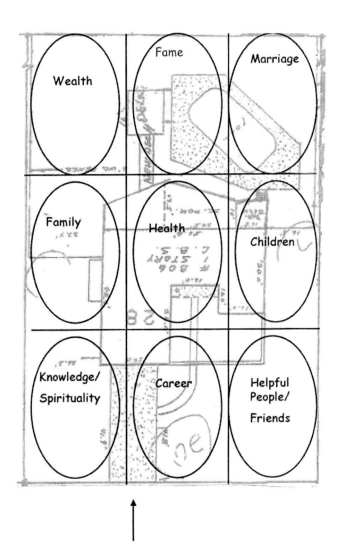

Extensions & Missing Pieces on the Bagua of your Land

If your lot shape is other than a square or rectangle, you may have extra energy in certain Bagua areas. This may provide you with more potential for fulfillment in that aspect of your life. Extensions are mostly beneficial. There are some rare occurrences where the extension is an over extension which can be too much and is likely to cause a struggle or imbalance. Extensions are generally a bit of good fortune and you do not need to make an adjustment to correct an imbalance.

This is how it works. If you have a piece of land where a piece extends out of the rectangle or square shape, it is an extension if this section sticking out is less than half of the that side of the land. Look at your lot plan. Then take your ruler and place it along the side where there is a piece sticking out of the box, if the total size of that side is 6 inches and 2.5 inches is sticking out, then it is an extension. 2.5 inches is less than half of 6. If the piece sticking out is less than half of the total side, then it is an extension or extra area of that Bagua piece.

See below the extension in Marriage/Partnerships/Relationships

Diagram #5:
Extra Marriage/
Partnership Bagua
on land

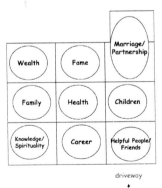

A **missing piece** is when less than half of the piece is missing on that side of the land. If you have the side to be six inches yet 4 inches is sticking out, then the 2 inch piece is actually missing. Look at the following example. You can see that the portion missing is less than half of the back wall. This makes it an obvious missing piece. Here is an example of a missing piece in Wealth.

Diagram #6: *Missing Wealth Bagua on land*

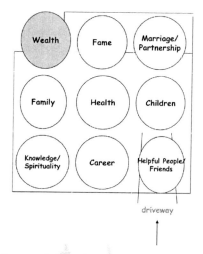

Once you understand the principles to place the Bagua map, you will easily know if you have missing pieces or extra enhancing spaces in your Bagua.

The above missing piece in wealth needs an adjustment. When you have a missing piece, there is a potential that it may be more challenging, difficult or impossible to achieve your dreams, needs and goals in this area of your life. Wealth can mean many things, primarily it has to do with being financially secure and prosperous. It is a basic instinct to have this sense of comfort. An imbalance can be to pull an 'Enron' and want so much that it is excess and it can backfire as well.

Wealth is about balancing time, energy and money while more importantly feeling rich, abundant and prosperous which has nothing to do with money.

Professor Lin Yun teaches and shares a poem he wrote on wealth -

Don't assume that seeking wealth
Is the same as being greedy.
Money just may bring relief
In hard times when you are needy.
Yet, if it is acquired and used
Without a proper method,
It will be easier to capsize a boat
Than to carry it afloat.

H.H. Grandmaster Lin Yun

When we have a missing piece in any area of your land, we want to make an adjustment so that the weakness potential can be corrected immediately and the chi is raised so it allows for the flow and ease of life achievements. On the inside of the property lines you can place a tall object like a flag pole, a light, mirror or plant a tree that is evergreen, bears fruit or flowers. It is wonderful when the leaves will grow upward. Windchimes are another choice. Moving objects are great. I have used large gazing balls, the modern outdoor mirror. Arrowheads can also be used. All of these choices and more will expand the property line. It is a great enhancement.

Whenever you have a missing piece in any part of the Bagua it is suggested to cure it. You do this by using a cure from the Basic Cure List on pages 62-64. Many parcels of land are rectangle in shape and have no missing pieces. It is more likely to have missing pieces on the home and the bedroom than on the land. Cure any and all missing pieces so you can reach your full potential with ease in that aspect of your life.

Special Lot Shapes and their meanings

We can have many different, interesting and unusual lot shapes. It is most auspicious to have the "Money Bag" shape. These are popular in the new community planning with cul-de-sacs. However, the contrary shape called the "Dust Bin" shape can be inauspicious. Special cures and adjustments can make sure that potential weakness is abated.

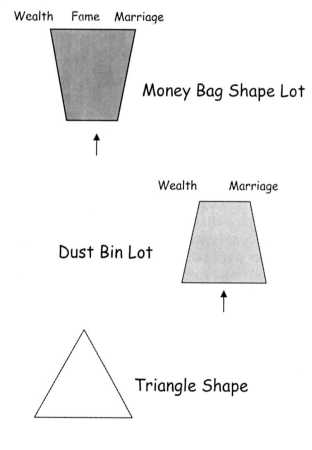

Money Bag Shape Lot

Dust Bin Lot

Triangle Shape

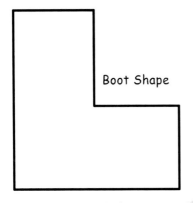

Boot Shape

The boot shape can be problematic. Depending on where the mouth of chi is – the door or entranceway – will determine where the potential problems may be. You can be in a position to be kicked around or stepped on. We will use mirrors to move the energy so that a weakness does not occur. If you place your bed, stove, or desk on a way that will be receiving the negative chi, it is recommended to place the mirror or move the bed or desk. As you look at this shape, the area on the bottom far right is considered the toe area of the boot.

Blade Shape

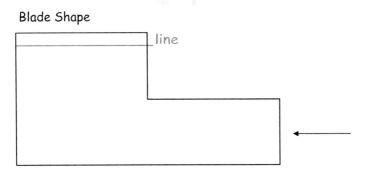

line

The arrow represents the mouth of chi. It is unusual to have this as a shape to land, but I see it very often with bedroom shapes. It can also be a shape of a second floor, office suite or hotel room.

If you place a bed, desk, stove on the side with the inside line, it can be a struggle and very problematic situation. If you cannot move your stove for instance you can place a mirror to offset the negative energy of it being on the blade, the cutting chi.

Placing the Bagua on the House

Wealth	Fame	Marriage/ Partnership
Family	Health	Children
Knowledge/ Spirituality	Career	Helpful People & Friends

Mouth of Chi, how you enter, front door, driveway, room door...

To place the Bagua on the house, you will begin at the mouth of chi, or the front door. So, if your front door is on the left hand side of the front of your house, the door will be in Knowledge/Spirituality. If the front door is in the center, it will be in Career. If the front door is on the right hand side, it will be in Helpful People. Sometimes the front door will be partially in one Bagua area and partially in another.

If you have a hand made sketch or an official floor plan, you will want to divide it up into 9 pieces, creating a tic tac toe board. The rules and method are the same as when you applied the Bagua to your land. Use your ruler again, and divide length wise and width wise by 3. In your nine boxes draw a circle. Then label each area according to where it lands in the Bagua. You will notice that each area may be partially a closet, part of a hallway and parts of rooms. If your house was 60 feet wide and 60 feet deep, each area of the Bagua will be 20 feet by 20 feet. It works this way, when you have a square or rectangular shaped house.

You will place the Bagua map over everything that is heated and air-conditioned. Decks, wrap around porches and other types of areas around the house are generally not considered part of the Bagua of the house. When you have an attached garage from which you can walk into your home without going outside, generally it is considered part of the Bagua of the house. There are many different scenarios that are considered on a case by case basis, and it is far too complicated to explain in the scope of this book.

Sometimes when there are screened in porches, Florida rooms, mud rooms and other attached unique parts of a home, they will be considered part of the Bagua, sometimes they are not. It really depends on each case. If they make up a missing piece, cure it. If it is an extension, enjoy the extra energy.

Let's look at a few examples of the Bagua on apartments and houses.

Diagram #7: *Bagua on Apartment*

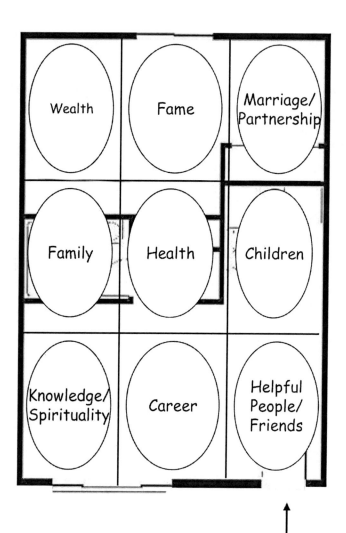

Diagram #8: *Bagua on Apartment*

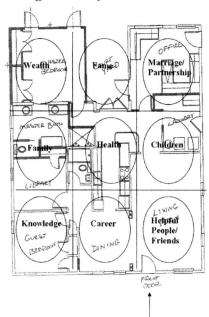

Diagram #9: *Bagua Placement on Home*

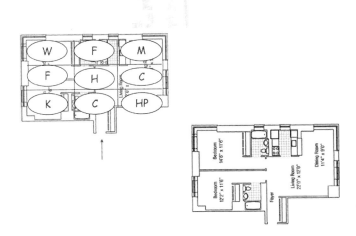

If your home is not a square or rectangular shape then you have a missing piece(s) and / or an extension (s). It all depends on how things map out. Any area that extends out from the house that is less than half of the length of that area, would be considered an extension. Extensions are mostly good. There are exceptions to every rule. If your extension is sticking out so far that it appears to be longer than half of the main body of the house, it can be too much of an extension. Translation - too much of a good thing can cause an imbalance. It may create so much energy that it may be difficult to fully enjoy. You can pull in the excess with a mirror. Mirrors are a great Feng Shui tool. There is a joke/cliché in the Feng Shui community, when a client calls in a panic late at night. We answer "Hang a mirror and call me in the morning!" Mirrors are used in many situations, we direct the mirror to move the chi as we intend it to be. It is quite simple, yet very powerful.

Technically speaking, if the piece in question is exactly one half it can go either way. It would depend on how it feels and looks. Everything looks different on paper than how it feels in real physical form, or in the 3D form. In every case I have experienced so far, we did adjustments for a missing piece when it was exactly half. Below are some examples.

Diagram #10:
Bagua on Apartment -
Missing Marriage

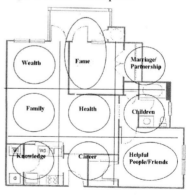

Diagram #11: *Bagua on House*

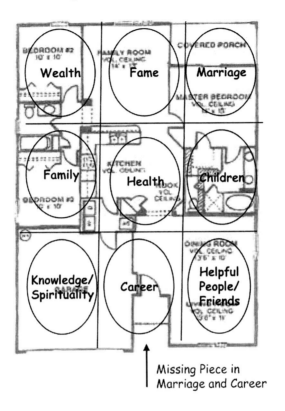

Missing Piece in
Marriage and Career

Cures for Missing Pieces in Homes

If you have a missing piece, it has the POTENTIAL to make that area not as fulfilling and/or enjoyable as the rest. You may have to work too hard at it. It may be too time consuming. You may struggle in some way. You may reach your potential, but at a high cost. The probability increases when you have another type of weakness in this area besides a missing piece. Or in another Bagua area, such as the land, home, or bedroom, if you are missing it too.

The great thing about BTB Feng Shui is that you can cure or adjust any imbalance. You do not have to move. You do not have to add on. Simply choose an energy adjustment that you will enjoy. It is best if you like the adjustment. Sometimes, I go in homes and people have placed something that they do not like at all and even call it a negative name. This is not 'great' Feng Shui. The adjustment can be functional and necessary to other needs of the home, business or organization that exists there. Choose something that you will enjoy its beauty so it will be the best Feng Shui for you. Choose something beautiful to your sense of style and design.

Mirrors are great to use. You can place one on either wall on the inside of the space. A mirror can be placed opposite the wall that needs to be energetically moved. The shiny part of the mirror is facing in the room. This will fill the missing piece. If you do not like mirrors or the area is entirely sliding glass doors, windows or you love how you have it decorated so much that you do not want to change the look at this moment in time. Choose something that you will like. Technically speaking, you can use anything from the basic cure list.

You can use a crystal, a round multi-faceted crystal ball. We use Swarovksi, as the quality is excellent. You can hang it in either window. You can hang it in either corner or on the point. *One cure is enough.* There is no need to do all or many of these unless you doubt it will work. However, you can do too much which can stop or confuse the chi. If you doubt it will work, you may not bother at all. Professor says, that doing Feng Shui without a sincere heart will not get the best results or any at all. You can go down the list of basic cures on pages 62-64, and choose a cure that works best for you and your home. We are adding energy. We are moving energy.

Outside your home is another area where you can make the adjustment to create balance in this area. Lights, windchimes and flags placed so the reflection or movement is projecting into the missing piece are more choices. You can create a function for the space. Perhaps a table for 2 in the partnership area is just what you will use and enjoy. You can plant flowers. Pink or red flowers will tie in with the Bagua color area for Marriage/Partnership.

At the place where you would square off the shape you can place something as well. Planting something beautiful may be perfect. Be mindful of just how big it will get and if it will receive appropriate light. There is much to consider. You can place a light in that spot. You may enjoy a bird bath, or a bird feeder, a waterfall and or pond or another type of garden feature. The varieties of adjustments you can use in Feng Shui are infinite. You could create something that has all five elements, or more than one type of adjustment. For instance, you can place on a shepherd's hook a windchime that has a crystal hanging from it in the center.

Extensions

So if the area that is not in the box is sticking out and it is less than one half of the side it is sticking out from, you have extra in that aspect of your life which can bring you good fortune or a way to reach your full potential. Remember Feng Shui is only part of your life and there are other factors to consider. Your fate, destiny, karma, education and accumulation of good deeds play an integral part in the happiness and success of your life.

Diagram #12: *Bagua on House - 3 Extensions*

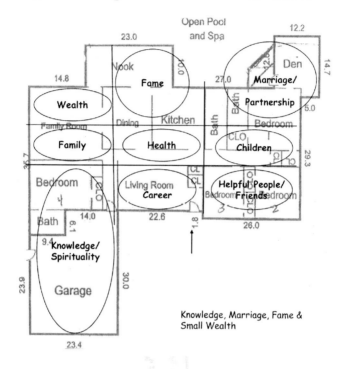

Knowledge, Marriage, Fame &
Small Wealth

The extension in knowledge here is actually an over extension. This can create "too" much information or energy and it may make it difficult to make decisions, comprehend things or simply enjoy your spirituality and knowledge in any way, shape or form. You can place a mirror at the end of the home in the family room to pull the energy in, so there is no longer an imbalance. If you wish, you can place a convex mirror on the end of the garage to again push the energy more inside the home to have balance.

Bagua on the 2ⁿᵈ floor of your Home

Second floors, basements and any other floors than the main floor also has its own Bagua. The 'mouth of chi' or beginning point of the Bagua begins at the entry to this level. The entry is at the landing of the stairs, or as you get off the elevator. At that location is the knowledge/spirituality, career, or helpful people. These levels usually have multiple missing pieces and extensions. There are so many different scenarios for this Bagua level, it is beyond the scope of this book.

Bagua Placement on your Bedroom

The most important place to overlay the Bagua is on your bedroom. You spend at least 1/3 of your life in this room, theoretically. You begin to place the Bagua at the door entering your bedroom. If you have doors that go outside from your bedroom, these are not used to overlay the Bagua. It is the door you enter your bedroom from the inside of the house.

Wealth	Fame	Marriage/ Partnership
Family	Health	Children
Knowledge	Career	Helpful People & Friends

Mouth of Chi, how you enter, front door, driveway, room door...

Below is an example of the Bagua placed on your bedroom. You can have missing pieces and extensions in your bedroom. I would use the cures and adjustment listed on pages 41-43 as described with missing pieces on your home.

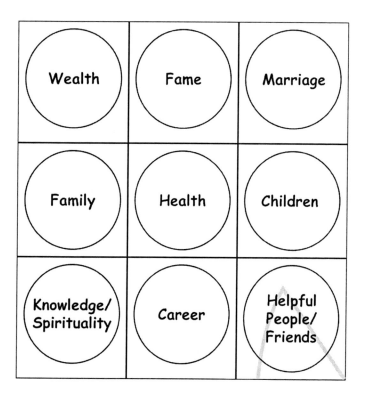

The Bagua is a very powerful tool. We place this over your bedroom because it is where you spend the most amount of time and where you rejuvenate your chi for your health and well being. As you enter the room, place your Bagua in front of you. You will enter in through Knowledge/Spirituality, Career or Helpful People. Sometimes a door is partially in Career and partially in Knowledge or Helpful People. However it is always on that side of the four walls of your room. Divide your room into a tic tac toe board, or divide by three, length wise and width wise. If your room is 15 feet by 18 feet, each part of the Bagua is 5 x 6. If your room is other than a square or rectangle, you will determine if you have a missing piece or an extension the same as you have done with your home and land. If the area that is outside of the box is less than one half of the side it extends from it is an extension. Most extensions are a positive characteristic of the Bagua placement on your bedroom.

Bagua Placement with a 'Blocked Entry'

Look at this example. As soon as you enter the door there is a wall and there is no house or part of the space to apply the Bagua to, on the other side of the wall. In this case only, you actually turn your body, then apply the Bagua to the space. In this example below, you will have a large extension in helpful people. Blocked entries most frequently occur on second floors, in apartments, condos, townhouses, villas and commercial properties. Placing a mirror, piece of art, or an aquarium, are a few choices to create a lively open feeling when you enter directly into a wall.

Diagram #13: **Blocked Entry**

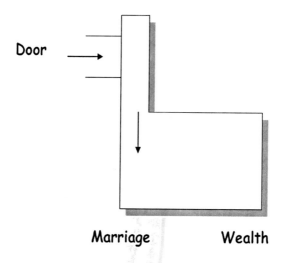

Door →

Marriage   **Wealth**

Angled Doors. When your mouth of chi is on an angle, to determine which way the Bagua is applied you must determine the flow of chi. It is based on how the door opens, how you enter the room and the furniture placement. In example A you can see that the pathway is directed one way, note where the wealth and marriage areas are located.

In example B of the same room you can see the pathway goes in another direction. Placing the Bagua is mostly based on the furniture placement as it determines the flow of the pathway, the flow of chi. It can be determined by the wear and tear of the carpet or flooring and the way the door opens. An angled door also has an imbalance of energy in regards to opportunities and how life's positives and negatives flow to you. You can place a crystal or windchime just inside or just outside the door.

Diagram #14: *Angle Door*

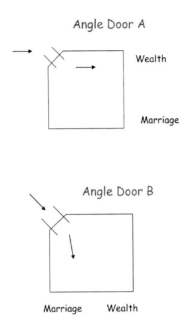

Technically speaking you can place the Bagua on any room, and it can be overwhelming and confusing to literally do so. The best rooms to place the Bagua on is your bedroom, each member of the house will have the Bagua placed on their individual bedrooms, the kitchen, and any other frequently used important rooms such as home office or study. It is not necessary to place the Bagua on your bathroom, or a walk in closet. It is actually not the most important energy components to those rooms. See more information on those rooms in chapter seven.

HOW DO WE USE THIS INFORMATION WELL?

In the next section, I will describe what each one of these areas mean in more detail. For now, let's look at wealth. Everyone likes a little extra money to save or play with.

When I work with the Bagua in regards to wealth, I want to check out the 3 main areas of wealth.

Look at the wealth of the land.

a. Do you have it? If not adjust for a missing piece asap.

b. What is the chi like? Do you have lush plants, trees or grass? Or is it filled with dead plants, or is it prone to flooding?

c. Can you get to it? Clear a path. Remove old or broken items.

d. Does it slope away? Place a cure to lift the chi.

e. Do you use it? Can you create a use for it.

f. Do you like it? To your eye of beauty, if not change it.

g. If you want to enhance wealth - add a positive producing energetic cure! Now! Do it with a sincere heart and visualize a huge flow of money coming into your hands to STAY. Or see your assets grow quickly.

h. Here are a few good wealth cure suggestions for the land. Place a purple flowering plant, tree or bush. Add a fruit tree or bush. Place a butterfly or bird attracting plants. Place 3 or 9. Add a water feature: waterfall, hot tub, Jacuzzi, fish pond,... etc. Add something that moves. Add a light reflecting back at the house. Place a flagpole. Plant some clumping bamboo. Plant an herb or vegetable garden. Place something to play with that all or many will enjoy. Place a shed. Place something with a prosperous symbolic meaning – a Buddha statue with a bagful of money, fish, a mosaic with all the colors, therefore all the possibilities,…. Etc.

Once you look at the wealth of the land, review the wealth area of your home. Ask yourself some similar questions.

a. Do you have it? If not adjust for a missing piece.
b. What kind of condition is it in? Enhance its vibration.
c. Do you like it? Do you use these areas?
d. If all is well, place an adjustment to add/ activate/ expand your wealth energy.
e. Choose so it blends well and you can you use it and like it.
f. Be specific with your wealth intention.
g. Mirrors are great. The bigger the better in this case.
h. Flutes, crystals, 10 coins, so many choices, just do it.
i. You can place a windchime off the edge of the house outside.
j. Water fountains are great here.
k. Wonderful art can be a very powerful adjustment.
l. Use purple, red, royal blue, green and rich hues if color can be beneficial in this space.
m. Make sure there is sufficient light.
n. Fix anything that is broken
o. Periodically pay attention to this space.

Most importantly let us look at the wealth of your bedroom. All the particulars of the bedroom will be addressed in the chapter on the bedroom.

a. Make sure you have the area of wealth in your bedroom. If not place an adjustment for the missing piece.
b. Do you like it?
c. What is there?

d. If your closet is not a walk-in closet your wealth may be in the closet. This can cause an imbalance. Do the cure to balance the closet energy. See the Chapter 7 on Rooms.

e. Add a very specific and powerful cure to the wealth of your bedroom, if you wish to have your wealth enhanced.

f. If you like music in the bedroom, place the stereo in the wealth area.

g. Select a cure meaningful to you from the Basic cure list on page 79-81, make your intention behind it very specific. You will be amazed at the results you will receive.

You can use a list to customize each area of the Bagua. If you are in the process of studying to get an advanced degree, or if knowledge is very important in your life right now, look at the knowledge of your home on the land, the house itself and most important your bedroom. If you do have an office or study in the home, I would definitely access the Feng Shui and add a special adjustment for your specific needs.

What do these areas of the Bagua mean?

The Bagua - What do these sections symbolize and how to use them well?

Each area depicts an aspect of your life. What is in these areas may be an exact mirror image as to what is going on in that facet of your life. For instance, if you have a lot of clutter in most of your home Knowledge area, it may be more challenging to learn or to experience a deep Spiritual connection with your higher power (God source, Buddha, Mohammed, universal energy, Love, however you connect with a Spiritual source).

Remember in the home itself, this may be parts of several

rooms, a whole room, a hallway or a closet or two. So, do not try to make every area do the function of the name of the area. BUT do look and feel the energy, as that is the essence that will carry over into your life. You do not have to study there. You do not have to have an office, library computer desk, prayer space, meditation room, altar space, sanctuary or any other room that is the direct function of the title of the area. It will have an impact on your life in regards to that life aspect.

I find the stronger influence of the Feng Shui comes when there is a pattern in the Bagua areas on several levels. Let's say you do have clutter in Knowledge/Spirituality of your home, and you are missing it in your bedroom, perhaps it is a closet and bathroom area upstairs and you are missing part of it on your land. Chances are very good that there will be a struggle to achieve your highest and best in this part of your life. If it does not happen immediately, you will feel the effect within one to five years of living in that space, Knowledge/Spirituality and all it means will cause some challenges in your life.

You do not have to move. Simply do the adjustments and recognize any life patterns that may need attention. Do your footwork or homework to enhance your weakness. Strengthen it. This is one of the beauties of Feng Shui. Do the Feng Shui and get busy. Intend, visualize, see and know that the weakness or imbalance is corrected so much that is works in your favor. Do activities daily or regularly that will help you attain your goal. Be mindful and take notice if you are doing something that is contrary to that goal.

What does **Knowledge/Spirituality** mean? It is what you know. Knowledge is information and data. It is how you use it, learn it and process it. It is about making good use of that information. This is how we make good judgments. Knowledge is also known as Cultivation, Contemplation,

Spirituality, and Judgment. It is your connection with the Divine (higher power, God, Buddha, ...). This connection gives you the inspiration on how to use your data. The trigram in this space is Mountain. Trigrams are the three lines that depict this area in the I-Ching, which is the basis of Feng Shui theory and practice. The I-Ching provides us with a lot of information about this area and all the areas of the Bagua. It relates physically to your body part of the hand and all that connects to your shoulder from your hand. Let us say, that you have carpal tunnel syndrome or tennis elbow that flares up and is very painful at times. Grandmaster Lin Yun has given us many tools to assist in your healing. First and foremost it is suggested that you go to another doctor if your healing is delayed. Try an alternative doctor or eastern medicine. Keep up the mundane work of getting well. You can also place a cure from the cure list. If you want a complete architectural and interior design detail list for this area, contact me directly. We also have special powerful cures that are Feng Shui and mystical remedies alike.

Family. Family is the relationship with your immediate family. Primarily your elders. It is a connection with those who you look up to with respect, those in authority. You can imagine all the associations and relationships this can represent in your life. The body part is foot. There are five elements in Feng Shui and the element in this area is wood. Knowing this can help you in healing with the five elements in the physical and emotional condition your personal chi is in. This means that the energy of wood is present. We like to balance our elements. It makes for good flow of chi in our bodies and minds. The five elements are wood, fire, earth, metal and water. It is wonderful to have 3 elements in balance or all 5 elements in balance. Wood feeds fire. Fire feeds earth. So, you can have 3 elements in proportion; wood, fire and earth. Wood chi has a direct relationship with your liver and gallbladder. You can use Feng Shui to help support healing in those areas if needed. The trigram is thunder.

Wealth. This area is a favorite of many. It does indeed symbolize our security, a sense of financial safety. Wealth is a connection of money, energy and time. To me, it is not helpful to you to expend all your energy and time making money, then you have less energy and will not enjoy the bounty of your money. Yes we want to have plenty in a balanced way. Wealth more importantly is feeling rich; rich in friends, joy, good health, loving family, and an overall contentment and peace. It is when one is not chasing to fill a hole inside that cannot be filled with fruits of money, or money itself. Wind is the trigram. To flow with the wind is ideal, rather than to constantly being at odds with it. The body part is the pelvis, your hips. It has to do with the male prostate as well.

Fame/Reputation. In ancient times, this was primarily about rank in society. This is not the be all and end all for life today on this planet, in most areas. Whenever someone (or a business) needs to be noticed this is the area to focus on. From an obvious standpoint if you wish to build your reputation or be famous, focus on this area. Celebrities, politicians and anything that will use public relations or savvy marketing efforts to launch or maintain its existence, will want to pay close attention to this area.

For most of us, it has to do with reputation, how you see yourself and how others see you. If your reputation needs assistance this is the area to remember. How do YOU SEE yourself? Is this a perfect match with how others see you? Sometimes people think more of the themselves than is true and other times people think less of themselves. It is a place to get an honest perspective. It also relates to vision. Your eyes. The element and trigram is fire. Be true to the fire or passion within is an aspect that can be experienced here. The eyes are the windows to the soul, you may use mirrors to help you to see what can be soulfully satisfying, your passion, a natural authentic experience of what you makes you happy. It will be to help you live your truth.

Marriage/Partnerships/Relationships -
This area relates to love, giving and receiving in relationships, partnerships and marriage. It is physical and emotional intimacy between two people. Primarily it is the husband and wife relationship, a special deep connection. It is the most yin area. The Trigram is Earth. You will see 3 broken lines on the I-Ching, or 3 yin lines. The body part is the abdomen, reproductive system. Love is here. How you love yourself prior to loving another is essential. Sharing Love, giving and receiving love. This area is so important to us. It has many properties that relate to mother earth. The earth is open, receptive, giving and vulnerable. These are some characteristics that happen to us when we are in love.

Children is the area that relates to your offspring. If you have no children, look at the child within along with children in your life, perhaps nieces and nephews. In today's society there are so many unique family environments. The element is metal. The health concern is the mouth. So it could be dental issues or anything connected to the mouth. Many times it has been referred to a connection with the future. Metal symbolizes your lungs.

The children area is an important area when one wants to conceive a child, or has had challenges carrying a child to term. Professor Lin Yun has passed on many powerful rituals that help people conceive and carry a health baby to life! The trigram is called lake. Children area is about joy and fun; ease and light heartedness. It is about seeing and enjoying life like a child.

Helpful People/Friends – Benefactors. The primary function of the area is to give back to others, to your community. Giving from the heart and generously without conditions is the focus of this area. It is a connection with your heavenly helpers. The Trigram is called heaven. It is the most masculine area. It relates to the Father and Brother.

You will see the trigram represented by 3 solid lines in the I-Ching. Solid lines are yang energy. It also relates to travel. If people want to travel more or if folks have fears about traveling this may be the place to balance and accentuate. This area also symbolizes your social connections and friends. It can be networking. When you need a good helpful mechanic, hair dresser... etc these areas are represented here. This area relates to friends, your circle of friends. Sometimes people want to expand this circle. Give to others, the earth, the community is the primary function of this area.

Career - this is your journey, your path in life. It is your foundation. It may be your job. It is how you fill your daily life. Your day to day activities. So for those of you who are retired, or not working this area still counts. It can be a space to focus on creating an incredible retirement. The body part is the ear. It can be your actual hearing, and how well you listen, or what you are listening to. The element here is water, and it is also the trigram. As the body relates to water, this area can also signify your kidneys, bladder or any issue that relates to water.

HEALTH - To me, this is the most important area. Without your health, everything else is less enjoyable and meaningful. It is a pivotal area, called the ming tang, Tai Chi – yin yang. Everything feeds into the center and the center feeds all the other areas. Overall health is in this space. Your overall health of your mind, body and spirit. If you have several areas of your health or life that need attention or help, you can do adjustments in this space. It is better to do Cures in this one space that to do it in many other areas.

Using the Bagua well.

When you want to add energy or change the energy in a particular area. It is best to check all the areas of that location. Wealth for instance. Make sure you have it on your land, in your home, your bedroom, your kitchen, and office. Make sure it is well. Do you like those areas? Are you using them? What kind of condition are they in. If you need to make a balancing adjustment do so first. Make sure the area is physically cleaned well. Use the space if it is not being used by anyone in your home. Then I would place an adjustment. You can choose the adjustment from the Mundane Cure List in the next chapter. If the energy needs light, use a cure that will provide light. Choose a cure that you like. Functional, practical, beautiful, meaningful to you are some of the adjectives you may consider when choosing a cure. Express your creative side. If you know a cure has a long history of use and meaning for the needed energy shift, this is an important determining factor of the choice of your cure. You can also make it yourself. It can be brand new. Size may matter. Timing of the placement of the cure will also add another meaningful element to your cure. Sincerity and positive heart felt intentions is probably the most important factor. Grandmaster Lin Yun has often said, four ounces of cure can move the mountain. If you believe, it is all possible. Feng Shui assists you to make shifts in your home and life.

Chapter 4
Basic Cures & Reinforcing Them

Below is a list of the basic cures and immediately following that is a brief description of each category. When you choose a cure take into consideration the energy that needs to be shifted and which type of cure would be most suitable to making that adjustment. There are many categories that are interchangeable and some that are not. To completely describe all the factors relating to the basic cure or mundane cure list would take an entire book, however, you will have plenty of information to make excellent use of these adjustments in your homes.

Hint: when you need to cure an imbalance a specific energy is usually needed. When all is well and you simply want to enhance or activate the area then any category will do. There are powerful transcendental methods that use these mundane cures to a deeper level.

Here is the list on Mundane Cures:

1. Light: Add bright objects
   • Mirrors
   • Crystal Balls (faceted)
   • Lights, Lamps (the brighter the better)
   • Others

2. Sound: Add something with clear sound
   • Brass Windchimes
   • Brass Bells
   • Other, (music)

3. Life Force, Vitality: Add something lively
   • Aquariums or Fish Bowls
   • Flowers and Plants (real or silk)
   • Bonsai
   • Others

4. Moving Objects: Add objects that move
   - Mobiles
   - Windsocks, whirligigs
   - Windmills
   - Weathervanes
   - Others

5. Heavy Objects: Add something with weight
   - Stones
   - Statues
   - Rock Gardens
   - Yu Bowl
   - Others

6. Power, Energy: Add something powerful
   - Firecrackers
   - Televisions. Air Conditioners
   - Arrowhead
   - Others

7. Color: Add something with color
   - Bagua Color Theory
   - Five Element Color Methods
   - Rainbow Spectrum
   - Six Colors of the true words
   - Others

8. Fragrance, Aroma
   - Oranges
   - Fresh Fragrant Flowers
   - Essential Oils
   - Other

9. Hydraulic Power: Add something with hydraulic power
   - Waterfalls
   - Water Fountains
   - Other

10. Other
- Chinese Bamboo Flute
- Ten Coins of the Ching Dynasty
- Beaded Curtain
- Zodiac charms
- Treasure Box
- Yearly Calendar
- Other

Light is essential. If you walk into any space and it looks or feels dark, it will be very difficult to keep high personal chi or environmental chi for very long. So, this may be the most important aspect of adjusting your space. You may use lighting to adjust your Feng Shui. Full spectrum lighting which is like natural daylight is very beneficial. You can lighten up a room or space by painting the walls a lighter color.

Mirrors are used very often in Feng Shui. I find that they go well with any décor and make for an easy fix or chi enhancer. Quality matters. To adjust Feng Shui, it is recommended to use a nice clear mirror; no black, tainted, antique, smoky, tinted or tile type mirrors. (you can use these type of mirrors for your design, just not for a cure, or Feng Shui adjustment) In some cases size can matter. Professor has often said, big mirror big cure. If it is impossible to place a nice sized mirror, make your intention large and clear. Shape can be beneficial on a deeper level. Round mirrors are great for the relationship, marriage and partnership areas for harmony and love. Oval can also be used here. Octagonal is for power, symbolic power of the I Ching. When you hang a mirror it is best if all people in the home can see themselves. Professor also likes us to be able to see our knees through the mirror in certain cures. In the BTB school of Feng Shui it can be advantageous to have a mirror in the bedroom. If however, if you feel uncomfortable or it does not agree with your chi at this time, I would cover the mirror while sleeping or remove it if possible. There are many transcendental cures for mirrors. The Bagua mirror is used generally above the front door for protection and to cure an imbalance with exterior factors beyond your control.

Crystals are used in Feng Shui for energy adjustments. We use round multi-faceted crystal balls that hang from the ceiling, a fan, in a window encasement, a car, over significant objects, or in the Bagua area needing a special enhancement. We can use them to disperse negative chi from architectural design factors that can be problematic. Crystals are also used to enhance any area. They are excellent for the health area of a room. You can use them in any Bagua area you wish to enhance. They direct the flow of chi. They are beautiful and can be used in conjunction with other cures or will many times fit in with your décor.

Size matters. 30mm crystals are great for small areas. 40mm can be an average size room size and height. The larger the space you want to adjust, the larger the crystal. 50mm for above average size room. 60mm or 70mm can be used in the center of a typical home. Larger sizes are also available. We will hang the crystal with a red ribbon or string, cutting this ribbon in a nine inch increment. It can be 9, 18, 27... etc. It can actually hang down 3 inches from the ceiling. You can add crystals to the end of your windchimes as an extra way to enhance the Feng Shui and adjustment.

Sound. Use when you want to adjust to move chi. Windchimes can be most powerful to attract energy, call forth a solution, clear energy, keep it high, activate an area, cure a missing piece and so much more. Chimes can be used inside a home. There are many powerful transcendental cures and uses of the windchime. Brass or metal generally make the best windchimes. Clear beautiful sound is very harmonious. You may consider listening to chimes before you purchase them.

Brass bells are another great chi mover. One bell can be used. Many bells on a string are also used. Bells can be a great adjustment at the front door. They are also wonderful in many offices. Door harps are lovely on the front door.

Gongs are great for space clearing, ceremonies and meditation spaces. They will clear energy from a space.

Music is fantastic for adjusting the chi of your homes. There are types of music that can raise the vibration as well as clear the vibration. Some are ancient energies and compositions of music, and some are newly developed and created. Quality is key here. What does the music invoke? How does it feel? The goal is to add positive energy or clear any negative energy, thereby raising the chi of a space. The possibilities are endless!

Life Force. Plants are very auspicious. They help us so much. Real plants are excellent to use. Good quality silk are fantastic. If you need fresh oxygen for the space or in addition to the cure, it is recommended to use live plants. Plants rising upward are wonderful. Fruit bearing and flowering plants are an excellent choice to add prosperity to any space. Three or nine are often recommended for a space. Two may be divine in the master bedroom or partnership area of the home. Too much in number or how it grows into seating areas or walk ways may be a detriment to chi flow and growth. Be mindful of how it will be in the area. Bonsai can be used.

Aquariums and fish bowls are both calming and auspicious. They are very good for wealth and health.

Flowers are used as a mundane cure. Real or silk are great chi enhancers. We also have a few transcendental cures using flowers. When you choose your flowers be mindful of the color, symbolic type, and how fragrant they are. You can use color as an added element to the flower cure. We also use flowers and fragrance to do chi adjustments.

Moving Objects. When you need movement, use this category of cures. Mobiles move chi, make or choose one that has personal or appropriate significance to the space, Bagua area or type of energy that is being moved. Wind-chimes are very beneficial. Whirligigs, windsocks, weather-vanes, windmills, flags, fans move chi. Once again choose a flag(weathervane, windsocks, etc) that fits you and your space as well as the energy you are moving. Any object that moves will help enhance the chi when you need movement.

Heavy Objects. When a Bagua area needs stability or weight in any fashion, place a heavy object or a symbolic object that looks as if it is heavy. You can also use this cure to block energy coming to your building. Stones, statues, rocks, sculptures, and Yu bowls can be used. Yu bowls are a mystical method and have several different transcendental purposes.

Power, Energy: When you need something powerful to energize or overcome an imbalance in an area of your life, you can place something with power or energy. You can reinforce it with the Three Secrets Reinforcements. You may already have an electrically powered object that is in regular use in your career area. It then may be able to move the chi on a deeper energetic level for your specific career intention. See the section on the Three Secrets.

For instance, let us say that your stereo is located in the Helpful People area of your home. Pick any aspect of helpful people that you wish to add more energy to, such as travel, friends, clients, heavenly helpers, a direction in which you should give back to your community, state, nation, world, or if you have a health challenge with headaches. During an auspicious day and time, use the intention process of the Three Secrets. Make a gesture with your hands (see page 63), say a prayer, affirmation or mantra you feel comfortable with, then imagine your life situation being enhanced. Imagine your headaches a thing of the past. Imagine giving to a worthy cause and how wonderful that feels. Pretend that you are traveling to your next place of interest. Feel the adventure in discovering and enjoying a whole new energy on this earth. Appreciate the shift. Feel the joy. Feel the gratitude. See it in a way that brings your heart to a smile.

Examples of powerful objects are Chinese firecrackers from Lin Yun Temple, they are blessed and for this use. You may also use other types of Chinese firecrackers that are a decoration. Place intention on your television, air conditioner, fans, stereos, lights and so on that are electrically powered. Use an arrowhead to shift the chi with power and clear direction.

Color: There are a few different ways to use color in Feng Shui. We have a color selection that relates to each Bagua area. Remember that color is one choice to enhance an area. If it does not match, work or fit with your design or taste, do not use the color of that Bagua even as an accent. Good Feng Shui you will love to see and feel. You can have excellent Feng Shui and never, ever use the color of the Bagua as a tool to enhance the chi. With that said, please be mindful with your selections of all your cures and adjustments.

Wealth's colors are purple, red, green, royal blue and even rich hues in general can be used here. Deep rich purple is the primary color for wealth. Fame's color is red. Marriage/Partnership's colors can be pink for unconditional love, red for passion (use in moderation) and white (not recommended to sleep in all white bedding and nightclothes). White has 2 meanings. One is purity. The other represents the clothing that one is buried in, or death. This is symbolic yet, I have seen cases with people who have dreams of death or progressive illnesses shift, when we remove all pure white and add some color the dreams stopped, and with proper medical care illnesses improved.

The Children area has the color of white. Helpful People/Friends Benefactors is gray or silver, then black or white. Career is black. Knowledge is a medium shade of blue. Family is green. Health in the center is yellow, and any earth-tone color.

You can also enhance an area by using all **Five Colors of the Five Elements**. It can be in the design or with a decorative object. A beautiful vase may be a choice. It can be a pillow or a piece of art. Get creative. Enjoy. The five elements are wood, fire, earth, metal and water. The corresponding colors are green, red, yellow, white and black. Professor has given us a healthy chi cultivation teaching to eat your meals with the colors of all five elements in mind. This can help to create and maintain balance or enhance your health. If you personally have an elemental imbalance then you can help your chi by adding more of the color of the element that will help balance and heal your chi. You obviously still go to your doctor. If you have too much of one element, you may consider using that color less and choosing a color that will be more supportive than depleting. This can be in terms of wearing the color. Using the color in your design of your personal spaces that you use frequently. You can eat more of that color. The Five Elements are a powerful contributing factor to the health of your body, mind and spirit. We have several meditation methods to help with healing.

Rainbow Spectrum. Using all the colors of the rainbow is a fantastic way to enhance a space. When you incorporate all colors, you can be open for all that life has to offer, or perhaps to help you reach your highest potential. This design is not limited to a picture of a rainbow. Create an object or view that has so many colors your imagination is lifted to new levels.

Six Colors of the six true words is a wonderful energy of high vibration and spiritual connection. The six true words are Om, Ma, Ni, Pad, Me, Hum. The corresponding colors are white, red, yellow, green, blue, black. The Yun Lin Temple has made many items with these colors; bracelets, necklaces, rings, added to crystals, spiritual secret transcendental cures, flags, and much more. The energy of those syllables is of a high frequency. I have been taught a few loose translations and meanings. It can mean 'the heart of the lotus jewel'. The deep meaning is the highest and best good. There is much to learn about this mantra and much benefit to be derived from its use.

Fragrance & Aroma. The most used in this style of Feng Shui is with fragrant flowers and the use of the orange peels for their scent and mystical properties. Whenever you smell the orange peel, it lifts your chi. There are many methods to enhance the chi of a home, person, business, room and Bagua area with flowers and orange essence.

In addition to using these BTB methods, there is a very profound and beneficial field of aromatherapy that is being used more and more today. The use of high quality essential oils is healing. Your olfactory system sends messages to your brain faster than any other system. You make a conscious and unconscious choice with this information without processing it for logic. It is amazing. I use many different uses of aroma in homes for health, real estate selling, wealth, harmony and love. When you get into some powerful essential oils the benefits are quite outstanding. This ancient wisdom has been passed down for centuries in many cultures and mediums other than Feng Shui. Study and apply for your highest good.

Hydraulic Power. Water fountains, waterfalls, moving water objects in pools and more are choices you may enjoy. Indoor water fountains have been quite an experience to use. Here are a few tips. Know that the pump does not last a lifetime, my experience is 12 to 24 months. When it gives out, do not throw it away, use it to find the proper replacement. If you know the exact model and size, search for it online or wherever. Not all pumps are the same size and shape. The indoor fountains recommend using distilled water, do that. Keep it clean. Take it all apart periodically and cleanout the gunk, dust and other matter from the air that makes it into the water.

Water fountains are great in Career and Wealth. They are fantastic just inside or just outside the front door. See it upon entering. I would avoid placing one in fame, as the energy of fire is there, and you can do it as long as the elements are balanced accurately. The stove has a great amount of fire energy – so placing a fountain in some kitchens may kick the elements out of balance. Lastly, avoid placing them where there is already a lot of water. Several times I have seen them placed in huge master bathrooms, and it really offset the energy. There is already plenty of water chi in a bathroom, when you add more it can cause an imbalance. Wood can balance too much water.

If you place a waterfall outside the front door, its flow should face the front door. Avoid placing it so that your neighbors will reap all the positive energy of water, while your chi will be depleted. You can also have a fountains' flow shoot straight up that way all are benefited and no one is depleted. There are many variables to consider here, but these are good fundamentals to begin with.

Moving water is best when it is clean. Consider this when you are placing them outdoors. I had a wonderful pond in my last home. There was a new easy solution to maintain algae without chemicals, an ultra violent light. It did not harm my fish and it kept the pond clean. Clean moving water is what you are creating here. If you cannot maintain this type of cure, you can add art or simply use another solution from the list of Basic Cures.

Other This category includes many of the mystical folklore and transcendental cures that Feng Shui has used for centuries. The Chinese Bamboo flute is made of real bamboo. The best one you can use is from the Temple, see *www.yunlintemple.org*. There are numerous reasons and places for this as a cure. The Bamboo flute symbolizes – peace, safety. It provides support. In the shape of a sword it may fight off an evil spirit. It has a powerful uprising force. The energy can help you climb upward step by step. You can use it as a pointer. It can be used to drive away a scoundrel. It can be used as a powerful health cure. You can place a bamboo flute in any gua. Use them to lift beams and chi of most any kind.

Ten coins from the Ch'ing Dynasty are a very special mystical cure. It can enhance wealth, career and act as a guardian in your home. These can also be obtained through the temple, see above website. The essence of this cure is quite simple, the coins are replicas of the most prosperous time from 1644 to 1911. It is a powerful wealth and career enhancer. There are numerous specific methods to use this prosperous energy.

Beaded curtains can be used to move the chi for our benefit. They are great separators of chi, and can serve as a door when you have an empty door.

The other category here can be endless. We have been given

hundreds of mystical cures from HH Grandmaster Lin Yun through the years. Many of these cures will serve you best when given individually from a dedicated student of Grandmaster Lin Yun, usually a disciple. You may be very fortunate and receive a cure directly from him. See where he is lecturing or teaching currently and go with plenty of red envelopes and give with a sincere heart. The cure you receive may change your life completely and may even be considered priceless.

Timing – Auspicious Days & Time

When you place your cures/adjustments/enhancements, the energy behind it is very important. Timing is important. Mindfulness and intention are key ingredients to the success of your shifting the chi. It is best to place cures on an auspicious day. These days can be found in the Chinese Almanac. Each day in each year will be different. The Chinese Almanac is based on eastern astrology and the lunar calendar. It is very scientific. Grandmaster Lin Yun has divined additional days that are deemed auspicious. The almanac also indicates very bad days otherwise known as PO days. They are described as days that are unsuitable for any activities. Avoid these days for doing cures and special events. If you have a special day, according to your culture, religion, western astrology, anniversary or other meaningful occasions, it is best to use that if the chi related to it is very high.

It is wise to place a bed, desk, front door, stove and dining room table on these days. There are many ways to make the best use of all the energy the universe has provided for us. This book is being released around September 2008 (another very Auspicious Time). If you are interested in obtaining the whole year of auspicious days, or for a clarification of an auspicious day for a special event, contact us at www.fengshui108.com. Here are the Auspicious Days for November 2008: 1, 2, 4, 8, 11, 12, 14, 15, 17, 20, 23, 24, 26, 27, 29. PO days for November 2008 are 13, 25. If you are interested in obtaining the remainder of the year, email us at *training@fengshui108.com*. Each year they are available for you.

If you use in depth the precise calculations of other astrology forms and have enjoyed much success with those, you may choose to use them for making your Feng Shui adjustments. Use the calculations and expertise of a dedicated and experienced astrologer to assist you in choosing your important dates.

We also like to choose the time of day to be around the noon or midnight hours. Between 11am and 1pm or between 11pm and 1am are the best two time periods. They are considered the most yang and yin respectively. Once again if your bio rhythm or any other hugely significant time of day is especially important to you or the cure you are doing, use that time period. The more components that create the special and reverent energy around the placement the better off you are to achieve the desired outcome.

Three Secrets Reinforcements

Three Secrets Reinforcements is the one component to Black Sect Feng Shui that makes it very powerful and effective. When you are placing your wind chime at the front door for instance, you will pause after it is secure and do the three secrets reinforcements. This gesture can be said to 'program', place intention, or create a powerful mind/body/speech connection to the energy you are creating. This act of mindfulness is often kept a secret from others for even more of the treasure chi to be created.

The body secret is when you make a gesture with your hands. Our hands speak volumes for us. It is a way that we let the universe know with a hand gesture way that we are honoring and energizing the Feng Shui. You can place your hands in a prayer position. Or you can use the heart calming mudra. This is accomplished by placing your left palm on top of your right palm and they face to the sky or ceiling. Your fingers lie on top of each other. Next let your 2 thumbs touch each other. Your hands can then be placed in front of your body; in front of your heart, solar plexus or your dan tien (a couple of inches below your navel). There are many types of mudras, gestures made with your hands. We also use the ousting/expelling mudra. A woman uses her right hand and a man uses his left. Your index finger and pinky finger extend out while your thumb touches your middle and ring finger nails. You will then flick your fingers up off your thumb. Generally you flick to the heavens or down to the earth. You can also flick straight at a wall or object you are directing the chi to be shifted. Generally you will flick 9 times. Trust your inspiration. If your hands want to clap, or be open to new opportunities as to offer a hug, use that intuitive nudge to customize the chi specifically to you at that place and time. In our future teachings we will discuss the many other mudras that exist in the Black Sect use of Feng Shui empowerments. There are many mudras to choose from and you may know one that is very special and sacred to you, use it!

The speech secret is used to state a prayer, mantra, affirmation or intended goal. You can speak it out loud or within your heart. We often use a Tibetan mantra (prayer), it has 6 syllables: Om Ma Ni Pad Me Hum. In many cases the precise translation cannot be achieved for we do not often have words and meanings that are equivalent. This mantra translates loosely to mean; the heart of the lotus jewel, or the highest and best good. It is very special and has been used for good blessings for thousands of years and chanted millions of times. If this is too 'foreign' for it to have sincere heart felt meaning, please use a prayer from your own faith.

Create a positive prayer or affirmation. 'Thy will be done', or 'bless this stove' or 'heal this space' may be more meaningful for you. If you are inspired sing a hymn or special song from your faith. We usually chant the mantra 9 times. (9 is a very significant number in Feng Shui. It is the strongest of the single digit odd numbers. It is yang and active.) I began counting gently with my fingers so that I could be in the flow. I will tap from my index finger to my pinky finger (4), then from the thumb to the pinky (5) making a total of 9. After some time using the 6 syllable chant I found myself chanting in the set of 3, three times, and a slight pause for more breath in-between each set of three. It flows harmoniously. It feels great and contributes to some very powerful and effective cures.

The mind secret perhaps is the most significant of the three. It also provides for the most individualized usage. You will then see the intended outcome happen. We all do this differently. So, imagine it complete. For instance, you have sold your house easily and for the precise amount of money you desired. If the picture does not pop in your mind's eye, you may assist your process by making out your deposit slip. Maybe you can draw the elation you will feel. Perhaps you can't see it with your sight, but you are flowing with the chi of victorious victory. You may feel compelled to speak the truth of your goal being achieved. Exclaim it. Radiate with it. Smile! Laugh! Feel the sensation of shear joy. Embrace your shift. Let your heart direct this secret. It is heart and soul driven not cerebrally created, unless you are drawing distinctively from your creative side of the brain. Regardless, dance your success feeling! We create this visualization differently. You may like to write it out. You can physically create it. You can draw it. You can speak it. Do what feels best for you. Some cures may require a different method by you. Use your inspiration. Enjoy!

Whenever possible it is best to do the Three Secret Reinforcements between the hours of 11am and 1pm or 11pm and 1am. It is considered to be the most yang and the most yin. You can place the cure or do the physical work in regard to the cure during other hours, but whenever possible do the empowering 3 secrets during these hours. If there is no way, I can reinforce during those hours, I do them immediately after doing the cure, and when there is a day and time when I am able to be fully present, joyful and not rushed, I will take the time to re-energize by doing the body, speech and mind sacred reinforcements again. Remember to honor your intuition and avoid fear or rigidity. Enjoy the creation of the chi you desire.

In using the sacred knowledge of the Three Secrets and Auspicious energies, we come to another powerful ritual that has been used for thousands of years, the red envelope. Since we regard Feng Shui as being sacred, it is very important to honor this tradition. It is fun to experience once you understand the nature and richness of its depth. The red envelope tradition is an important energy empowerment technique that we use to enhance your Feng Shui and to keep the energy high, when honoring this custom, both the practitioner and the recipient of the information will be empowered, blessed or receive good luck or fortune. Generally speaking, when you receive a special cure it is best to honor the teacher and give her or him one or more red envelopes with money in each red envelope. The amount can be left up to the recipient of information unless it is a secret method, then the practitioner will let you know how many red envelopes and how much money should be placed in envelope. Here is a full description of this valuable tool.

Red Envelopes, Value & Transcendental Cures

This whole concept is different, ancient and foreign to us today. So, while I explain please have an open mind and think with your heart energy.

Red envelopes symbolize value, honor and respect. When a Feng Shui Practitioner trained by His Holiness Grandmaster Lin Yun or someone deeply under his tutelage asks you for red envelopes it is for your greater good as well as theirs. This mystical practice is rich in positive energy. This method brings reverence to the giving and receiving process. (hard to take it for granted when you take the time to do this!) You appreciate it more!

It connects us to this ancient practice and all the successful uses of it now and in the past. The lineage of this work is very powerful and special.

It creates a more special and sacred way to change the energy you have in your home, business and self. It enhances and enriches the entire experience. This special empowerment is rich in custom and tradition yet it is a signal to the universe that you are ready to receive the good that will come from the information received.

When you receive one simple cure, or adjustment it is customary to give one red envelope. It generally is not the fee for the information given to you by the expert. In this red envelope you can place a token of money of any value. *What is most important is the act of giving from your heart.* The amount is not as important as the significance of doing this ritual. It is said that it can be more valuable when a poor person puts a dollar in it, than when a millionaire puts a dollar in it. It is reverence and value of the Feng Shui work and the person who provides that to you, which is invaluable, so the custom was created. The empowerment and blessings of the envelopes is given and received from this context. So all aspects of giving them is relevant, not just what is put in them. People sometimes make envelopes, create artistic positive messages on them too. It is also said that if you take the time and energy to locate them or prepare them ahead of time is also a way to make the energy more special.

When there are more complicated cures, even for one cure, it will require more energy, therefore more envelopes. Consider this an honor to do. The more you give the better it is. Consultations are usually 9 or 27 envelopes. Chi adjustments start with 27 envelopes. Involved cases, on a rare occasion can take 108 envelopes. Some powerful chi moving methods alone are 27 red envelopes. Trust that the lineage is dictating this and it makes the transfer of energy all the more beneficial.

The practitioner will regard these envelopes as sacred. She/he will usually not open them until the next day after a meditation and offering for your intentions. Sometimes they will not open them for 3, 9 or 27 days. Most practitioners donate part or all of the money received in the red envelopes. Some use the money for expenses to help people in need with Feng Shui and other gifts.

There are other uses for red envelopes in the Chinese culture. People usually give new dollar bills on New Years Day to children and single people. It is also a tradition to give money in red envelopes to a bride and groom as a wedding gift, or as a gesture of good fortune and joy for the marriage. I have given gifts to people who provide services for me. I have also mailed my mortgage in a stationary style red envelope. Years ago, I stopped giving out candy on Halloween and began using spare change in red envelopes to give to the children in the neighborhood.

So enjoy the ritual of giving and receiving the red envelope!

Just last year we noticed an additional note in the back of the notebooks we would purchase for the class. It said that if the content of the cures work for you to send nine red envelopes to Yun Lin Temple at 2959 Russell St., Berkeley, CA 94705, USA. You can always send more if so inspired. The power and energy of connecting with this lineage is very special. You can if you wish send red envelopes to the author of this book, when your cures work for you. If you wish more advanced cures, contact Kathy Mann and she will help you with the appropriate cures. In order to receive the more transcendental methods, red envelopes are necessary. Her address is PO Box 20683, Tampa, FL 33622, or website *www.fengshui108.com* or phone 813-388-1300. There are volumes of information available for your needs and wants.

Chapter 5
Position, Position, Position

In the Black Sect style of Feng Shui we are not concerned with absolute direction when choosing a home, placing a bed, placing the front door and all other major Feng Shui principles. The emphasis is position in relation to chi flow. Chi flows into a home through the front door. Positioning this way benefits all persons in the home. We call it 'the commanding position.'

Your bed is the most important piece of furniture. When you place your bed, it is best if you can see the door easily while you are lying in bed.

It is not suggested to place your bed in direct alignment with the door that you use to enter the room. This means that if you were lying in bed your feet would be directly lined up with the door. The best way to describe this, if you walk in the door and continue straight ahead you would bump into the bed. This position is referred to as the coffin position. You are in position to be taken out to go directly into your coffin. When your bed is not directly opposite the door, you do not have this situation. (I have been asked this question a lot)

It is highly suggested that your bed is in the position furthest place in the room from the door, so that you can see all that is before you, the entire room. This position is called the 'commanding position'. It is empowering. Since ancient times, emperors, leaders and people in control have coveted this position in office buildings, villages, battle fields and all types of competitive arenas. It is the ideal place to hold court. The symbolic representation gives you the edge to having the best position in life. Let your environment give you an edge in life, so you can see all that is before you.

Bed positioning a,b,c's.
      a. Place the bed in the furthest position from the door entering into the room.

b. Be sure to see the door or entrance into the bedroom.

c. Do not have the bed in direct alignment with the door entering into the room.

d. If you feel sensitive to a window behind your head (especially without a headboard) do not place your bed with a window behind you.

These abc's can be applied to your desk, the stove and objects that are important and meaningful to your life, work or home. When your fax machine is important to your livelihood, place it in a commanding position. The two most important factors is to be able to see the door (chi flow of energy into your life) and to not be in direct alignment with it. When in direct alignment, there can be too much chi and can weaken you from any and all standpoints.

When you see the door, it empowers you. Symbolically in your life you see the path you are on and you know what to change when the flow changes, or take a better road. There will be ups and downs in life, yet this will give you less of an upset or down time when things are not as smooth. When you do not see the door, anything can change at any moment without a blink of notice. You may get a flat tire and it could be hours to fix it, yet when you see the door, it may be a very quick fix. When you can't see the door too many things may happen behind your back. There may be back stabbing. This positioning practice of Feng Shui dates back to form school, it is quite nice to have a mountain behind your back, a solid wall in the interior space, you have a wonderful way to position yourself.

Another factor about sitting or sleeping with your back to the opening of chi flow or door, is comfort and best use of your energy. On a subconscious level, even in the comfort of your own home, you will wonder when you will be startled or surprised. This can set up your body and mind to be on edge on a subtle yet real level. You will expend more energy with stress when you do not need to give yourself that depletion of chi. It could even affect your sleep. So, a good rule of thumb is to make sure you can see the door. If you cannot physically see the door, you may place a mirror on an angle so you can see it perfectly. A recommendation here is to use a bedroom stand up dressing mirror that is oval, so that both people in the master bed can easily see the door. There are many creative ways to accomplish this with different sizes of mirrors. Think of basic geometry or the game of pool, you can place a mirror so it can be effortless to see the door. Positioning any mirror on an angle is usually the best way to accomplish this empowerment.

Diagram #15: *Bed Position in Room*

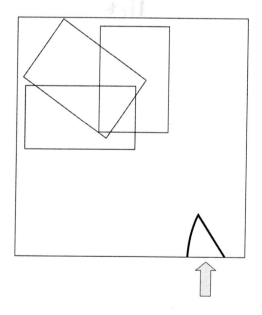

Chapter 6
Master Bedroom Position in Home, Floor plan

Position for your bedroom in the floor plan of your home is also important. Look back at the Bagua map. (see page 26). It is highly auspicious to have your bedroom in the marriage or wealth area of your home. It is most beneficial to be located behind the mid point of your home. If from the front door to the back of the house it is 50 feet long, anywhere behind the 25 foot mark is the best position for the master bedroom. This places you in a position of power, the captain of the ship. It is the position for the King and/or Queen of the castle. Please take whatever life style you are in and adjust my metaphor. You are the leader of the ship, head of the household. You guide, direct and nourish your children. You are responsible for them. There is a balance of power and chi when the head of the household is in the furthest position from the front door. Remember there is always a way to adjust this imbalance.

Here is an example of an imbalance of energy. Imagine that the head(s) of the household are sleeping in the knowledge gua while the children are in wealth. The potential imbalance is that the child may feel responsible for the home in some way. The child may have such a strong voice, or needs may be so consuming that it depletes all the chi out of the parents. It is recommended if you have an emergency as a passenger on an airplane that the parent take the oxygen mask first, then help the child. This way your chi is being nourished by positioning well, so you can take very good care of your child and that your life is in balance.

To cure this imbalance, you can place a mirror in the parent's bedroom that will reflect their chi into the back of the house, so far that it is behind the child. The intention is that the parents are fully able to support, direct, guide, teach, nourish and raise the child. The child then knows the parents are behind them 100% while having a deep respect for that authority and leadership. Bear in mind all the details of the multiple causes and effects of energy. This works well when the mundane or actual life choices of all the parties involved support the intention. Using the power of the parent's actual presence in the day to day life is just as important as the symbolic Feng Shui positioning strategies. Not all of us have children to care for at home, this relates to having a balance, harmony, manageability and direction in your own life. If a home office or guest room is in the power position work or guests may take energetic advantage.

Your Bedroom

This room is the most important room and space for you. Theoretically you spend the most amount of your time here than in any other place. One third of your life is this place, you are still, quietly taking in all of the environment from every sense and energy level. So everything around you affects you tremendously. Your bed is the most important piece of furniture. Quality and placement are crucial to providing you great chi all night long for the wonderful rest so upon awakening you are fresh and rejuvenated.

Enjoy your interior design. Love it. Like it a lot! I call this room for partners, the no sacrifice zone, no compromise zone. If you love blue, and he hates it, please do not put blue in your bedroom. This goes for all kinds of décor objects, type of sheets, types of pillows, and how the room is taken care of. Both of you should love the feel and design of the room, co-create it. Be mindful of what you place and where. It should connect with you and your partnership. Beauty from your eye that speaks of serenity and love is the vibe in this room.

The purpose of the room is primarily for *sleeping*. This space provides you with the main place for nurturing your relationship, intimate time, making love. So the vibe in the room is best if it is relaxing, calming, peaceful, etc, while still havng a connection to your romantic relationship. So it can be sensual, erotic and/or give it personal symbolism, to your union as a couple. What I mean by this is, if you enjoy a passion together, let us say the beach. Use a photo or piece of art that depicts your favorite beach, or you two on the beach joyful, blissful and/or peaceful. The meaning is for you two not the whole planet. If you do yoga together and that is how you met, perhaps a sculpture or piece of art of two bodies intertwined in yoga positions might be something that will create a positive loving vibe. You can of course, place things that symbolize your closeness and love without a literal or past connection. What is most important here is that you like it, and it has a heart felt connection or beauty that you BOTH enjoy. Avoid overly feminine or too masculine, for instance, lots of dolls or art of a battle scene. I have seen both. Practice artful mindfulness.

Avoid exercise machines, fax machines, desks, computers, mini libraries, and other pieces that are not part of the purpose of the room. In very large bedrooms, some exceptions are made when we can section off the other uses of the room. If the object does not support sleep or making love, it does not belong in the bedroom.

Bed placement. Your bed is best if it is placed so while you are in bed you can see the door, while it is the furthest place from the door entering in to the room, while not being in direct line with the door. See diagram 15 on page 84.

If you are in line with the door and cannot avoid it, then you can place an object that will hang from the ceiling in-between the door and the bed. Use a Swarovksi crystal. You can use a windchime, a mobile or any other object you will enjoy seeing. It can hang a short distance from the ceiling, however the red string you hang it on should be cut in a 9" denomination. It can be 9", 18", 27" and so on. If you prefer use centimeters or a system of measure that you can make the cut to be in a nine section, or multiple thereof.

If you have a window behind your headboard and you feel like your chi is vulnerable to be pulled outside, place a crystal from the window to stop the chi from pulling your energy out. Not everyone has that sensation. The more solid wooden headboard and the larger the distance between your head and the window, the more that it will not be an issue.

Headboards. They are excellent to have. A headboard symbolizes support in life. A beautiful solid wooden head board is generally best. Metal headboards may have issues with electromagnetic fields. These fields may be charged when created, or in the shipping process, or when they arrive in your home. Data and information about any kind of negative side effect or by-products that are expelled from our cell phones, wireless computer fields and the other new technological advances is not known completely. Side affects are still being debated and researched. Some research has indicated there can be harmful effects. Until we know enough information, keep as many electromagnetic fields out of the bedroom especially close to your head. If you are sleeping with a metal headboard and have an unusual, progressive or debilitating illness, I strongly urge you to change headboards. At least test it out. Switch it to see if you feel better. It certainly cannot hurt. Do your own research. As always, Professor tells us to remember if it is not broken do not fix it, so to speak. If things are going fine health wise and people feel well supported, I would not make a change. Listen to your body. Some of my clients like to have their head face in a certain direction, some north, some east. By all means, listen to your body and intuition first and foremost. Then, I would make the necessary adjustments to be able to see the door.

Keep it simple. In the décor of your bedroom, use a mix of 3 colors, maybe a fourth, but nothing more than that. Patterns should be kept to a minimum as well. It is not calming to see stripes on the window treatments, paisley on the bed, while you have wall paper with little diamond shapes. It can be way too much, even if the colors are pastel or light shades. Too many patterns can have a sense of too much movement which is not recommended in this space of calm relaxing sleep. The focal point or most attractive and attention getting piece should be your bed as you enter. This is most enjoyable if it is not overdone as well. Unless you love taking off a dozen or more pillows to go to sleep, I would avoid a large amount of pillows and things you do not need to sleep on the bed. Sometimes art works over a bed, sometimes it competes with the beauty of the bed. When you enter your bedroom, your respiration rate should slow down. You are being embraced by the creation of beauty, peacefulness and sensual calming essence you have infused in this most special space.

Colors. Different colors can invoke different energies. Most importantly is that you love the colors. Avoid intense, high frequency hues as your main color. Green and pink relate to your heart. Pink is a color of unconditional love. This can be quite beneficial in a bedroom to nurture a relationship or to help create a new one. There are several transcendental and mystical cures that use pink to help with relationships. This does not mean that the bedroom needs to be pink in color.

Touches of red are fantastic for sparking passion in your relationship. Blue can be a calming color. Most of all choose colors that will lift your spirit, or bring you joy without adding too much energy in a room that is mostly used for sleeping, avoid using multiple patterns or design. Peach is a color that has a Chinese folklore meaning which is not good for fidelity. It can be used to attract but not to keep a relationship. It is called Peach Blossom Luck.

Art. Choose your art wisely. Choose art to bring more beauty, calmness and love energy into this very special place. I have been in master bedrooms, where the couple has fully decorated the entire home and 'never got around' to choosing art for their bedroom. Your bedroom is the most important room in the house and can definitely affect your chi in all aspects of your life and relationship. You may need help in choosing art. A great designer can be most beneficial here.

For the best sleep and good health, close your closet doors and door to the master bathroom while sleeping. The chi in the bedroom is to replenish, while the bathroom chi is to let go and release what we no longer need. In Florida, and other parts of the world where humidity is high, closing a bathroom door after a hot bath or shower may not be a wise choice due to mold and mildew issues. Every situation is different. With excellent aeration systems, it may not be an issue. However, if you do heat up or steam up your bathroom right before bed, I would not close the door all the way. This is another example of customizing Feng Shui to the person, place and time. Another situation where it does not matter to close the master bathroom door while sleeping, is the placement, distance and pathway between the bed and the commode. The closer and more direct the connection, generally it is most necessary to close the master bathroom door.

For great sleep keep the least amount of things around your head, especially electromagnetic objects. This is especially a concern if there is a book shelf as the headboard. Keep it simple. If you need a backup alarm clock, do not put it next to your head on your nightstand. Place it across the room, or at the very least on the other side of the nightstand. Do not charge up your cell phones in the bedroom, especially next to your head. If you like a sound machine, or music machines plug them in as far away from the bed as possible. Use a remote control to turn off and on. Keep it simple with books and reading material too. I have seen dozens of periodicals in piles next where someone's head rests in bed. This can influence a poor sleep. Heavy subject matter can also be problematic to a sound peaceful sleep. Underneath the bed is not a closet. Keep it free and clear whenever possible, especially if you are not sleeping well. Let's say you have 8 inches from the bottom of your bed and the floor. If you have a two inch object that can simply lie flat and it fits absolutely no where else and you are healthy and sleeping well, I make exceptions. Keep the energy clear under the bed where you head rests.

There are many things that can affect great rest. Each person on this planet is affected by energies differently at different times. First things first, make sure your bed is of good quality, and is not ready to be replaced. If you sleep on a high quality mattress nearly every night, it will wear quicker than if you travel a lot or live in more than one home. The bed is the most important piece of furniture that contributes to your personal energy; your health, attitude, ability to work, think and enjoy life. Choose well. When new technology comes out, let it be tested first before you jump in with both feet. Excellent quality bedding is highly recommended. All cotton is not the same, as is with all other fabrics. Go for less number of sheet sets. Instead of quantity choose very high quality, your body will thank you for it.

Be mindful of what you first see in the morning and what you last see at night. Let it lift your chi, nurture you. Fresh flowers are excellent in the bedroom. Live, lush plants are a natural chi enhancer, while providing you with fresh oxygen all night long. Plants are very healing and symbolize growth, positive life force energy. High quality silk are beneficial too, obviously it does not provide fresh oxygen but can symbolically provide all the other attributes mentioned. I have clients who do not like or enjoy silk plants and others who for many reasons find it impractical to have live plants. Use aromatherapy to enhance the chi of this room. I like to make a mixture of Bergamot, Lavender and Rose oils or skip the rose and use Ylang-Ylang. I clean with citrus oils, mostly orange. Vanilla is a great oil to be used here for romance.

Mirrors in the bedroom are viewed differently by the various schools of Feng Shui. Trust your intuition, your mind, body and spirit. Grandmaster Lin Yun has taught us to read the chi of the client. Many of my clients love mirrors in the bedroom. Some are uncomfortable with them. Mirrors create lots of different types of energy. If a mirror reflects its their energy at this time and place, it may affect your sleep. Rarely do I see this as the true culprit of sleep deprivation. Sometimes if a person is going through a challenge in life, a health condition or during the grief process, it may be best to cover the mirror. If you are not sleeping well or through the night, rule out or decide if the mirror is contributing, cover it while you sleep. You can place a blanket, scarf or sheet over the portion of the mirror that reflects your head. Sometimes, if it is on a dresser, I have suggested to place one of those extra decorative pillows in front of the mirror thereby eliminating the reflection.

If you are waking up at night, before you sleep make an intention that when you wake up you will focus on the contributing environment factor. This may show up in you seeing it, sensing it, smelling it, or knowing what it is that is affecting your excellent quality sleep. If you are not used to working with this form of mindfulness, you may have to try it a few times.

Here are some things you can check for if you are not sleeping through the night. Lots of stuff under the bed, clutter, too many things near your head, bathroom door open, door into bedroom open – giving a view from bed clear into other room(s), toilet behind the wall where your headboard is, closet doors open, poor quality bed, poor quality bedding, electromagnetic fields in the room or on the other side of the headboard, poor pillows, whatever is exactly above the room where you sleep, whatever is below your bedroom exactly, plumbing pipes behind the headboard in that wall, too many patterns in the design of the room, too many pictures of people looking at the bed, disturbing or distracting art, too much reminder of the past where grief is involved, too much dust or not clean environment, and so on. In order to find out if one of these things is contributing to you not sleeping well, adjust it so that issue is not present, or do a transcendental cure and you will know what the cause is.

Here are a few client examples:

- A child realized it was one of his toys, how it 'pointed' at the bed. When it was moved, great sleep by all was achieved.
- A woman explained that her neighbor who worked until 2 am, would set off the motion lights between 2:30 and 3:00 am, which reflected in her bedroom and sent the light into her mirror. So it was not her mirror but the lights. Light darkening shades and curtains was all that was needed. Great sleep was created.
- Clutter. A woman discovered how overwhelmed she was with all the 'stuff' in her bedroom. Under her bed was full of legal documents of unfinished business problems. Sleep followed a clutter cleaning.
- A couple realized that when they kept the door opened, they could see two other rooms, so they closed the door halfway so their pets could come and go, yet they did not wake up any more.

Placing cures in your bedroom and in-between your mattress and box spring are the most influential on your chi in nearly all Feng Shui situations. (Remember if there is a block or negative influence of chi at the front door, it will limit the chi that can give you energy in all aspects of your life and environment)

If your relationship needs some healing or positive energy, focus on the marriage/partnership area of your bedroom and bed. Your house and land are also important, however where you spend the most amount of time will affect you the most.

Bagua Placement on the Bed.

This is how you place the Bagua on the bed. The foot of the bed is where you line up Knowledge/Spirituality, Career and Helpful People/Friends.

Review the list of Basic cures on pages 62-64, see the numerous examples for cures you might be interested in. Using the energy of the bed to place your cures is probably the most powerful place for you to enhance your life.

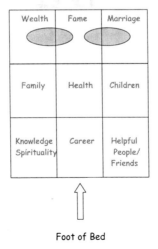

Foot of Bed

Obviously, small items will be placed in-between the mattress and box spring, yet the closeness to your chi is quite empowering. There are many sacred, secret of the secrets cures that His Holiness Grandmaster Lin Yun has given us in recent years that make very good use of this space.

Use your sincere heart when placing your cures. See your intentions come true, feel the joy and gratitude you have for these gifts and life in general.

Chapter 7
Rooms

The *Kitchen*. This room is very important for the health, wealth and career of everyone in the home. Your stove is one of the top three items in your home. Placement of the stove is very important. Placement of the kitchen and its stove in the floor plan is another key factor to use when choosing a new home. A full study on this is available in another book. For your help now, here are the key factors to consider.

The kitchen should be light and airy. A dark kitchen can be problematic on many levels, so if the kitchen appears dark after a remodel, even if the quality of the upgrades are high end, place adequate lighting to offset the dark colors and wherever possible paint or use light colored wall paper... etc with your interior design touches. If possible, place a mirror that will reflect natural light from a window that gets sun.

Design for beauty, simplicity and efficient use of your food preparation and cooking tools. Watch clutter; your counter tops do not need to be filled completely. Have out those gadgets you use daily or nearly daily. If you have a bread maker out that you use once a year, it can create stagnant chi, or it will simply be in the way. Store the rarely used bread maker off the counter top. Things change. Sometimes people use things seasonally or go through phases, flow with your needs and design. It should change periodically.

Color in the kitchen tends to be in mostly solid shades. All solids with no design or pattern can sometimes give a flat feeling to a kitchen. Using a colorful plate, piece of art or useful tool in corners or scantly placed around the room you will add vitality. Using only one color or similar tones of one colors can create a flat energy, infuse with colorful energy. If you use the color red in a kitchen that is located in wealth in a home, it may not be positive for wealth. I would avoid decorating with red in this case.

Too many patterns can also cause an imbalance. For instance, I have seen square tiles, diagonal backsplashes, and long rectangle lines on cabinet design in several forms on one cabinet, along with stripes in wall paper. It was too chaotic. Too many pictures on the refrigerator may also lose the appeal of enjoying photos of family and friends. Less is more.

Your stove is a symbol of health, wealth and career. Use it. Keep it in great working order. Rotate the use of your burners. All of the burners can be seen as a potential stream of revenue, a way to enhance your wealth. Whenever you can place a mirror behind the stove, you will have several benefits. You can see behind you while you are cooking, which is very empowering. Whenever you can use the laws of bed and desk placement it is ideal, this is hard to achieve, so the mirror is the cure. Any mirror which reflects the burners is a wealth enhancer. It can double your wealth. This can be achieved on either side of the stove, or even across the room. Mirrors add light. I have seen this done beautifully. One mirror is sufficient, however more done tastefully can be most financially beneficial.

Foyer. It is nice to have a foyer, not essential in great Feng Shui. If you have a foyer, the most important energy to feel is that it is well lit and open upon entry. If it feels dark upon entry you may feel uncomfortable. Make it so the light goes on automatically as you enter. You can also do this so a beautiful sound goes on as you enter. It can be music or the sound of a brass windchime is auspicious. A tight constricted space, seemingly or literally is also something to avoid. Keep this area light beautiful and simple. Mirrors may make smaller spaces appear larger. Be mindful to place the least amount of obstructing objects around the first few steps as you enter and along the general pathway into the body of the house. A water feature or art is a good choice here. Shoes kept by the door should be orderly. If not there can be particular struggles over time that could easily be avoided.

Living Room/Great Room/Family Room. In this space it is best to have furniture positioned so that family and friends can gather, communicate and enjoy each other, not just to stare at the television screen. In many cases the focal point tends to be the TV, an outdoor view or a fireplace. We can create spaces where you can see each other using a semi-circle, horseshoe shape, or the letter c shape with furniture so that you can easily enjoy the circle of friends while watching the TV together or the great view or tremendous fire. To make it very inviting make sure there is a wide enough opening so that you and others who will enter this space have adequate space to easily enter. If you have to move sideways, or climb over the magazine rack, or try very hard to avoid bumping your leg into a piece of furniture, it is not ideal. If you stand with your arms by your side and move them parallel to your body in a swinging fashion as you can saunter into the room, this is a wide enough space. If you are smaller in stature than the average person, make your adjustments accordingly. This way when you are moving about quickly on automatic pilot, you and your furniture or decorations will not collide. This will help create a most inviting place for your family, friends and other guests.

Colors can be many and in several patterns and designs, unlike the feel of the bedroom. This room is very active. Art can be dramatic, thought provoking, inspiring and energizing. These are general thoughts on the living room/family room/great room or whatever you call the family gathering space for other than eating. If for some reason it is imperative to create a space that is more calming, please do so. Make it attractive and beautiful.

Dining Room This room is very important. It symbolizes career. Eating at a dining room table other than one or two holidays a year is suggested. If you have a formal dining room, please use it. Whenever you have any room or rooms or floors in your house that go unused for long periods of time, it can create a flat, stale or dormant energy in that area of the Bagua and/or with the energy or purpose of that room. So, find a reason to make use of this space.

In your every day eating table, whether it is the kitchen table or dining room table, it is important to eat together as a family. It helps keeps harmony in the family and money in the home. For couples, it is great for your relationship and your finances. For a single person, it has an affect on your finances. Adorn the table with fresh flowers for wealth, career and harmony in the family. You can also place a mirror underneath it. Avoid beams over the dining room table. Avoid seeing the dining room table from the front door. Adjust these two conditions with cures if you have them in your home.

Bathrooms. These wonderful conveniences of modern times have gotten a bad rap through the Feng Shui grapevine. I love bathrooms! Modern plumbing is a pleasure to use. In some places in the world, they are considered a luxury, so appreciate them. They are an every day tool, so make them pleasant to be in. They are necessary and very easy to use. They symbolize 'letting go'. We cleanse our bodies and eliminate toxins, very necessary functions. Letting go on a symbolic and spiritual level is also helpful to stay healthy and keep your chi high.

It is not suggested to have a commode dead center of your home, or in the health area. There are tons of cures to cure this weakness. It is not recommended to have the commode in the wealth corner of your home. Also, it is not advisable to have one on the exact other side of the wall from your stove, or bed, or desk. One placed directly above the front door should also be avoided. Since you cannot move the commode (unless you have excess cash and lots of tolerance and time for contractors), there are plenty of cures to offset this imbalance of chi. One way is to place a mirror on the door going into the bathroom.

The master bathroom door is suggested to be closed while you sleep. Think of this, when you are sleeping you are rejuvenating or replenishing, taking in energy. The bathroom is where you let go. Opposites, right. I want to separate this energy. The more space between the bed and the commode especially, the happier I am. I have seen numerous suggestions to keep all drains and bathroom doors closed all the time. Not. I live in Florida presently. We have high levels of humidity. It is important to make sure you have an even air flow and drying up of moisture of all kinds in the bathroom especially. If you close a bathroom door, after a nice hot bath or shower, it does not allow for a smooth quick drying of the moisture. This can create mold and mildew in any climate. So, if you are going to jump into bed after a lovely hot bath, do not shut the door in a humid climate.

Please take the time to really study the environment you are working with before making a change so that it is most suitable for that space and time. This is one of the best things about BTB Feng Shui. Consider all the variables to enhanced balance the chi for the best Feng Shui. It is only then, you will create the environment that is most suitable, while having a high positive vibration, and is beautiful, functional and comfortable to those people for that place, time and purpose.

Walk in Closets. Flow of chi and ease of finding what you are looking for is the objective. Let your things breathe. Let go of those things you don't need. A walk in closet of a master bedroom is not part of the Bagua of the bedroom. It is mute to place a Bagua map on the walk in closet itself. Mirrors are a great Feng Shui addition to a walk in closet. They can symbolize keeping an eye on your stuff, or making sure you don't forgot about that aspect of the Bagua of the house. This may be important in areas that are near and dear to your heart. Place something that moves, even if ever so slightly as it hangs from the ceiling may be another great choice.

I have seen many people in Florida place fans especially if there is not a large air vent in the closet, it makes a big difference. We are avoiding stagnation of energy. Overall, do not overfill any closet. Leave some space. Tightness of chi should be avoided. If there is a situation where things will stay still for a long time and not moved over a year (in some cases 6 months) move your stuff, dust and clean well, them place it back. When you do this, take a moment to decide if you still need to 'hold' onto these things. Can they be used to fulfillment somewhere else. See the writing on clutter (page 115) to help with these choices.

Garages. And attached garages in many homes are closets for extra stuff and the car, they become a foyer for the occupants of the home. Think about that. It is how you are being greeted as you enter your home. How does that feel? How are you storing your stuff? If you have to do a mini obstacle course to enter you home, that can equate to struggle or simply giving yourself a hard time, a real pain in the neck. Even non-believers of Feng Shui get this. Give yourself a special entry. It is worth the energy, time and money to make this work. You will receive a benefit from this on a deep level each and every day.

What do you see as you enter from the driver's seat in your car, suv or mini van. If you can keep that view simple, that is great. For instance, cabinets are wonderful. If your optic nerve can see 20 things versus 200 plus things, I am happy, your chi will be happy. If you have shelves, can you cover them with fabric or install cabinets? Can you place your items in non-clear containers, so you actually see way less. Be mindful to keep the color all the same, or only use 2 or 3 colors of containers. Less is more here on many levels.

From your car door and all those who will travel with you, make sure you have a nice wide path. Place carpet runners if possible. Make your entry comfortable and special. This is important. If you are carrying bags, children, flowers and so on, make sure you have plenty of room. Keep the trash out of the pathway.

Can you paint the door coming into the house a different color? Can you place a poster, or beautiful poster of art, wall paper art, on or around the door, so that your eyes will focus on that and not all the stuff that makes you think of chores, etc? Play with what you have to create a warm, fun, lively greeting so when you come home you smile inside, instantly. Place a decent door mat. You can make this area feel good, by observing it differently, and making the appropriate changes so it is clear, clean, attractive in the areas that serve you as a entranceway, or 'foyer'.

By nature of garages we forget about them. Does the garage itself need a little cleaning? Perhaps let go of items not used in quite some time, or duplicates purchased for whatever reason.

By the way, your garage interior color does not have to be white, grey or beige; try yellow, green, purple, blue or whatever you enjoy! If this room has become your foyer, enhance it. Be mindful of what you first see when you enter the home. I see laundry rooms or narrow hallways. Place something beautiful to be the first viewed spot. Keep light and airy. Watch for chemical cleaning smells, litter boxes or other types of trash to be the odor as you enter.

Guest Rooms. Bed positioning may not be as important if not in use very often. Make sure the room does not become stagnant, never used just collecting dust. If you have run out of space for active areas of your life hobbies, interests and needs, you may consider using the guest room space for this activity, if you rarely use it. Maybe it could have a dual purpose. It is best to use all of your home to its fullest potential.

Laundry Rooms. Design the space so that it is highly functional while adding a little color, art, or whimsy. It is a routine chore. The laundry room does not have to be grey, white or beige. Cabinets are wonderful. Keep it light airy and easy to use. Watch overuse as storage, especially if it interferes with an easy use on a regular basis. Place whimsical art or posters, or something that will make you laugh as you enter.

Chapter 8
A Few Architectural Details

By no means is this a complete teaching of architectural details. There are many to teach. Below are a few that can be more common. My experience with Feng Shui consulting is that using the Bagua, assessing the chi of key areas in regards to interior design, the chi of the land and the architectural nuances are the fundamental levels of Feng Shui. When there is a pattern of the same weakness of chi or potential for less than optimum energy, I see it on several levels of energy. This book serves as an introductory guide to enhancing your chi and that of your home. The imbalances usually show up in the Bagua (on more that one Bagua overlay), and one or two of the other energy levels: such as chi of land, history of the location, interior design, and architecture design. Here are some common examples.

Windows represent the energy of the children, your eyes, the future and provide good natural light energy in a home. The playful chi of the window meaning and the mere fact of day dreaming out of the windows, may be the logic behind it if we have too many windows in a room you may not accomplish as much study or work. The size and location will matter. The number of windows in relation to the number of doors and size of the room will also be taken into consideration. A loose rule of thumb is that if there are more than three windows to a door, it may be too much. We can make adjustments to keep the energy more stable if necessary. One can use crystals, mirrors, heavy objects or an artistic door like feature.

Did you know that if you cannot see out the windows in your home because they begin higher than you can see, it may create a sense of a loss of freedom and a sense of being controlled. Placing a mirror in that room can offset that predisposition of energy.

Doors represent opportunity, symbolize the adult getting things done. They also represent your voice, how you communicate. They bring energy into a space. So much can be said about doors. The two most important doors in your home are your front door and the door to your bedroom. Review the information on the front door in chapter two. Be mindful to make sure they work well and are not obstructed. When a door squeaks lubricate it with wd40 or any other product that will be helpful. If there are too many doors in a small space especially without windows, things may be too serious, too many opinions, possible arguing and not enough fun. You cannot add a window, but you may be able to bring light to the situation with a mirror, a crystal, or perhaps some beautiful art work. Door sizes and shapes as well as how they are lined up with one another and how the chi flows in and around your home can bring may different interpretations of chi. They are quite important. Sliding glass doors are generally viewed as part door and part window. Depending on where they are located in the Bagua, use and your current life situation will determine if a cure is needed.

Stairways bring energy to and from different levels in your home. We like them to have risers. What they meet at the level can help or hinder the movement of chi into that space or out of that space. For instance, when the stairway is lined up with a front door, it is a potential leak of energy flowing right out the front door. There are plenty of cures to stop the flow of life force out of the home. If the space between the front door and the stairway is more than 12 feet, it may not be an issue. The closer it is the more of a concern it is. You can hang a crystal. Place mirrors on either side or above the door. You could even place one on the door. If there is enough space, furniture may be helpful. Place things that you enjoy seeing and that are functional for the space.

If your bedroom door on the second floor meets with the stair way to go downstairs, it could mean a weakness of chi. Place a crystal in-between the door and the stair landing. Dark and narrow stairways can also create a substantial chi weakness.

Spiral staircases make it challenging to have a smooth chi flow from floor to floor. They are especially problematic in the health area of the home. Plants underneath are helpful. There are many methods to help the energy to flow.

When you come into a blank wall, you can add a mirror to open up the energy. Art placed that is light bright and expansive may also be quite uplifting. Much of the Feng Shui principles make a lot of common sense. You may recall when you land onto a space with a short distance and a blank wall. It is not inviting and feels stifling. You may even feel your energy constrict.

Slanted walls or ceilings can create unexpected, unfortunate events to occur often. Cures are mirrors and bamboo flutes. All can be shifted for a more positive and pleasant experience.

Beams have been written about a lot in Feng Shui. In the deeper studies with Grandmaster Lin Yun, we take into consideration all aspects of the room before determining if the beams need an adjustment. How high are the ceilings? How wide are the beams? What color are the beams? A very dark brown beam on a white or cream colored ceiling with a 7 or 8 foot ceiling will definitely need a cure.

Be mindful of beams over the front door, your bed, the stove, the dining room table or your desk. We use traditional and modern interior design techniques to adjust the chi. If a beam is truly oppressive, simply painting it a lighter color so that it is flush with the color of the rest of the ceiling may be sufficient. You can also use Bamboo flutes, crystals, lights, and red fringe. Feng Shui gives you choices to make the enhancements you need.

Fireplaces whether in use or not have a tremendous energy of fire which can cause an imbalance in any Bagua area. It may be especially problematic if it is in the position of an extension in a Bagua area. In the Health area it can severely affect health.

There are numerous ways to balance the energy. The two elements that will balance fire are water and earth. Earth is what a fire produces. Water will put out or soften the fire. Fire can also melt metal. All of these interactions will soften the amount of the blaze. Wood will feed the fire. A mirror above a fireplace is a symbol of water and can balance the chi. Placing a piece of art that contains a lot of water is another way to do it. An earth element object can be in what it is made of, the color or the shape. Many times fireplaces are made of stone, brick, marble or some other material made from the earth. There are many ways to balance the fireplace energy.

Chapter 8
Interior Design Thoughts

We use many interior design methods to balance Feng Shui energies. Examples of this are throughout the entire book. Feng Shui is not an interior design style. Feng Shui can be used in French Provincial, Modern, American Country, Italian, Eclectic, and even the college dorm look. Feng Shui's purpose is not to become a style, yet to work with yours to make sure the vibration is working for you, not against you.

Interior Design is an art unto itself. Design your home from your Heart. Do what you really like/love. Beauty is in the eye of the beholder. Good Feng Shui is beautiful from your eye as well. I am not an interior designer, nor is it my aspiration to become one. Choose your color, art and so on from what you love. Using an interior designer to pull it together may be quite beneficial, if the beauty from your eye is fully understood. Personal style and comfort are key elements to creating the right Feng Shui for you.

If you think in terms of the purpose and needs you have for a particular room or space, then design from that. Trends come and go. You may enjoy changing things periodically. Design for how you live and what you need and want. Let your space provide for you on every level. Be mindful of trends. A few years back there was a big trend to use a lot of red in Dining Rooms. This was not a good idea. In any eating area, having a very intense fire color is not good for harmony or excellent digestion. If you add it to a household that already has passionate people, it may ignite fighting. So, trends come and go, think through a new idea. Imagine it in the area that you use and how will it play out.

Using a professional interior designer to help you create a look combined with your Feng Shui knowledge is an excellent idea. I am amazed at the knowledge and gifts great designers have to create beauty. Use Feng Shui with that expertise and you will love your home!

Real Clutter

Perception can create individual definitions for things like clutter. Look at both ends of the spectrum for a moment. On one end is the very neat barely any knick knacks, can't have a glass on the table for 60 seconds longer than in use extreme view of no clutter. To the other end, where there is stuff everywhere, you walk over piles of clothes, books, papers and more in a day to day existence. In this case the extreme is so out of control, that anyone would have a hard time changing that pattern. Most people exist in the middle. People go to extremes for a reason. Usually there is a deep rooted reason for the control or lack thereof. I have avoided teaching on this at a basic class level since most people have been fed this perception that a little pile or two is clutter. Feng Shui is not about perfection, rigidity or living in either extreme circumstance.

We usually hold onto to 'stuff' for a reason. It could be a issue with imbalance with one of the five elements. It could be a holding for comfort, i.e. like the pacie, pacifier. I am in that category, the thumb sucker. I love clothes, blankets, and a few other things. Once upon a time, I practiced a little retail therapy. Anyway, through practice it has stopped. This did fill a hole for a while anyway.

The other major reason for holding onto a lot of things, is illogical but it is connected to security. If you have 20 wooden spoons, or 20 hammers unconsciously you may feel that you will always have money for the rent, mortgage and to pay the taxes. Financial security, more is better.

Letting go of either of the 2 root clutter issues, or any other clutter issue may take time to acknowledge the feelings that were avoided in the first place. When I work with a woman who has ended a major chapter in her life through death, divorce or empty nest syndrome, it is not advisable to stop the comfy clutter immediately or all at once. Taking small steps is advisable.

When I started to let go of my clothes, I was told to let go of anything I had not worn in a year. That was too intense. I chose to do 2.5 to 3 years. I had the now I can let go pile, the maybe later pile and the no way ever going to let go pile. Eventually nearly everything that I could not really enjoy or wear left the house. I had to learn to trust that I would still have pretty comfortable things. When I worked with paper data (pre-computers), if I needed to locate information I had to trust that I could find it easily.

If you create spaces in your home for your things and set realistic limits to how much you can house or enjoy at once you will feel comfortable with your things. If you do not love something why keep it. If it does not provide something for you, *it is taking something from you*. You may be simply paying good money to store it. Energetically it can be draining. A good bottom line approach is do you love it or use it? Do you need to keep it for documentation purposes? If your answer is no to these three concepts, why are you keeping it. Make a commitment to own your things, do not let them own you or waste your precious energy.

True real clutter is when you have no idea what you have, where it is, many unfinished things and perhaps all over the place, it is in your face and you feel bothered by it. If you really have it, it can affect you negatively.

Real Clutter Can...
- Stop the smooth flow of energy in a space.
- Create undesirable symbols.
- Create excess baggage.
- Depress you, cause disharmony
- Put your life on hold
- Make you feel ashamed
- Make you procrastinate
- Affect the way people treat you
- Confuse you
- Affect your body weight
- Congest your body
- Keep you in past
- Make you feel tired & lethargic....
  Etc, etc, etc

Chime Cure - Place a windchime over the clutter. Ring it 9 times. Visualize that the clutter is lifted and the real issue is resolved and removing the clutter is an easy non-draining task. Take one item, place it where it belongs and go have fun. Within a short period of time the overwhelming clutter will be removed.

If you are the type of person who needs assistance organizing things to prevent clutter, ask for help. Maybe you have a friend who is great at this type of organizing. If not, hire a professional. Try the below method and make your own parameters for getting rid of the clutter.

Clear clutter for good. Make a game out of it. Create your own parameters ask yourself the questions that will push you I you used this item? Did it fit, work well, ... etc. How many do I have and how many do I really need? Let go. Let someone else use it. Sell it. Give it away to a shelter. Give it to a special friend or family member. Be free.

Everyone is different, Just Do it:

- all at once or step by step
- make the commitment
- anytime is the best time
- make it a game, play beat the clock and see it disappear.
- use aromatherapy, orange peels, orange or citrus oil, peppermint, or eucalyptus in the congested space so it does not deplete your energy.
- use Space clearing bells to disperse its hold on you before you spend time doing it.
- process your emotions, be gentle, and yet move with it.
- make a list of clutter zones
- get boxes to sort, label each —- trash, repairs, transit, yard sales, recycle, dilemma, charity, selling, ...etc
- hire a professional organizer.
- Begin small
- Treat yourself with each effort.

***Reminder: Clutter does not appear on its own. Habits make clutter. Work on changing the habit that creates your favorite clutter. There is clutter in your schedule as well. Balance your time with organization and precision! Emphasis is on progress, it takes time to create new habits that you enjoy, reward yourself. If clutter has been an issue for a long time, it is more than likely an element out of balance, do an assessment with 5 elements of a person and do the appropriate cures. The cures will balance the chi and stop the cause for the continuing use of clutter.

Release clutter before doing Cures!!! Clean before doing cures... In some cases this may not be the feasible. Do cures to move the chi. Remember Feng Shui is not rigid. Just Do it now!!! Prepare your space for the new positive energy and vitality. If you can't get past the clutter, a clearing or chi adjustment is best first. This is best when done by a trained professional.

Chapter 10
Working with the Invisible

Energy is all around us. In some cases land, homes and buildings hold positive energy and/or not so positive energy. All energy can be changed. Energy can be moved. Some energy gets stuck. Old stale, negative energy should be moved out, even if your personal energy is high, you may be weighted down. In some extreme cases, there can be very dark negative energy. If a space has that energy, it is best if a trained Feng Shui Practitioner or trained space healer. There are authentic ways to protect yourself from the dark energy.

His Holiness Grandmaster Lin Yun has taught many methods to do Chi Adjustments. Many people use the name space clearing. A fundamental method is called 'Tracing the Nine Stars'. It uses a very special ancient path to walk through a space to bless and clear energy. I use this method in many homes. It is easy to use when you are in a hotel room. Use the connection to your own faith or spiritual inclinations and get yourself centered. Ask the God of your understanding, your Buddha, Jesus, Mother Mary, Mohammed, Kuan Yin, Angels, your Creator, the Universe, Blessed Beings, Your Deity, Higher Power…etc to fill your heart and mind. You can say your prayers, mantras, sing hymns, …etc. Ask your Deity of choice to bless your space with and for you. Think about the intention of what you are doing. I will often state that any energy that is not in alignment or for the highest and best good of all the occupants of the space will be given the energy to vacate the space. In addition, let the space and all the people who reside in it be blessed with love, light, great health, wealth and all kinds of good fortune for their highest and best good. Many times after getting centered and in a prayerful state the words, prayers and mantras that are special for that time, space and people will easily flow with love and joy.

Do the chi adjustment on an auspicious day and time whenever possible (see chapter four). Open all the windows and doors whenever possible. Begin in the Family area. Make it a very special occasion. Light an unscented white candle. Ring space clearing bells. Buy some beautiful fresh highly scented flowers. You can play wonderful spiritual music. You can also use the element of fragrance. Burn sage or incense. Use essential oils. Thank the space for its service to you. Thank your Deity, Buddha, Angels, God,…etc and/or Guides for being present and doing the energy adjustment with you (for you). In the BTB Feng Shui practice we use a mantra that is called the six true words. "Om Ma Ni Pad Me Hum" is chanted nine times to clear and nine times to bless. We first clear any unwanted, negative, stuck or energy that is in anyway not in alignment with you to leave, we give it a vehicle or mode of transportation to leave. We use the expelling mudra, flicking nine times. You can also have your hands in prayer. Ring your bells or waft your sage or incense. Visualize all negative energy vacates the premises. Ask it with love to go to a place where it will be in balance and harmony with all the energy in and around it. Ask your higher power, Buddha or whatever you call your connecting spiritual energy, to assist in the transition. Let go of any negative past experience you may have experienced in the home. See every particle of negative energy leave the home at once.

After you feel that is complete, I would then use the expelling mudra to bless the space with all positive energy. Bless it with love, good fortune and all the energy that will support you and your family in your time in this home. Chant the mantra. Sing praise. Ask and feel the blessing. Feel the joy. Know that you will prosper and enjoy your home, life, health, wealth, relationship and career. Please be specific to your needs. Thank your home for the comfort of the shelter and great energy it is supplying you. Honor it by thanking it for all the joy you can experience. See the blessings ahead and at this precise moment as special gifts that bring you joy, laughter and much good fortune. Share this energy with your neighbors and send it out to the entire community, country and planet. See the love envelop the earth and go out into the vast universe. Magnify the good, loving energy you are planting. These seeds can grow. Please use language and words from your faith, heart and soul. Ring your bells, tingshas, gongs, and other vehicles of sound that will raise the vibration of the space. Use fragrance.

You can now see the visualization of this aspect of your life being blessed. The Family area and all that it means to you. See harmony, love and good fortune for your entire family. If there is a specific intention for healing or extra energy in this part of the Bagua, see that blessed. For instance, the foot is the body part affiliated with this part of the Bagua. If you have sore feet, or simply wish that your feet will carry you to the next wonderful chapter in your life, do it. Let your inspiration guide you. When it feels right, leave this area and go the next area on the below diagram.

Your path will be Family, Wealth, Health, Helpful People/Friends, Children, Knowledge/Spirituality, Fame, Career and you will finish in Marriage/Partnership. This path is very powerful and sacred.

Tracing the Nine Stars

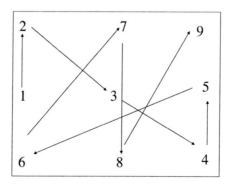

Chapter 11
Special Cures & Methods for You

Most Important – Health

In studying health and Feng Shui using the Black Sect Methods there are layers of how health can be supported and affected in a negative way. Each part of the Bagua has a body part. Some have an underlying layer of health descriptions with the five elements, which are only in different areas. Then there is a relationship with the systems that provide comfort, such as water, electric, heat and so on have another layer of impact. Architecture and interior design have an impact as well. So, even though the center space is health, it is overall health and is definitely used to create a positive energy space to support your health and well being, it is not the only area where you will look to the design and overall energy to uplift and accentuate to help support a health condition or state of being.

The Bagua areas each have a body part that corresponds to it. Family is the foot, wealth is the pelvic area and prostate, fame is eyes, marriage is abdomen and reproductive organs, children is mouth, helpful people and friends is the head, career is the ear, and knowledge is the hand and does include up the arm to shoulders.

Here is an example of the process I go through to thoroughly explore a health condition a client may have. A client has migraines. This can show up in helpful people as that is where the head is located. It can also be influenced by the front door. Depending on the root cause of the migraine, it can be the next way to examine the Feng Shui. If it relates to allergies, I may look in the Children area as it relates to the lungs from the elemental standpoint. I will also look to make sure there are no poison arrows facing my client while he or she sleeps. I will check the Health area to see if there are depleting elements or energies there such as the stove, toilet or fireplace. Your head can relate to the roof, as it is the top of the house. If all is in balance, maybe I will suggest she/he sleep in yellow sheets for healing or perhaps to do a mystical cure or meditation. Perhaps the air quality needs to be checked, for if it is not in great condition it may be the cause of the migraines. This is the beginning of the work.

Many mystical methods are available for you see in the appendix how you can acquire the information on a particular conditions or illness. We would be happy to help you. The list of health condition far exceeds one hundred. Some ailments are grouped into categories in regard to systems.

If someone is very ill and there are many different conditions you look to the center of the house for placement of the cures. Mystical cures like the Three Flute Method can be placed in the bed, in-between the mattress and box spring. There are many ways to influence the energy in a positive way.

Wealth

Wealth is a hot topic with Feng Shui. I have had many clients have tremendous success using Grandmaster Lin Yun's knowledge. You will create the change with the information you learn. It is ultimately up to you.

There are many visible, traditional and mystical cures on wealth. It is a vital human instinct that gives one a sense of security and balance. You can use the Bagua color, Chinese coins, Bamboo Flutes, Treasure box cure, 3 legged frog, water fountains, fish, aquariums ... etc. The list is endless. Do cures in three locations. Land, home itself and the bedroom are three usual levels. Paying attention to your wealth areas without addressing the energy of the front door may or may not work. Each Bagua area has a 180 degree partner which influences it. Helpful people/friends/benefactors is the area where you give back.

You give to your neighbors, friends, family and community without the notion of a return. Giving without conditions or strings, it is giving from the heart. Sometimes the leak of wealth is not in wealth but in helpful people. Make sure there is no missing piece or major problems with the energy in helpful people. We have also learned in recent teachings from His Holiness Grandmaster Lin Yun that the Gua before the Gua you wish to enhance has an energetic impact as well.

When you choose a cure, a large clear mirror is very powerful for instance. When you place the cure, and use the Three Secrets be specific in your intention.

Relationships/Love/Partnerships/Marriage

We have numerous visible and mystical methods to create, heal and enhance relationships. Cure any missing piece. Heal any past relationships completely before you use Feng Shui to assist you in the manifestation of a new healthy happy relationship. Forgive yourself. Forgive all of your former spouses/lovers/partners whatever your significant other is called.

To create a new relationship, heal the past. You can place a round mirror in the marriage area. Place a wish list of the type of love you want to draw into your life on pink paper in a red envelope and place it in the marriage area of the bed. Reinforce with the three secrets reinforcements. Place something that speaks of partnerships, especially one that has meaning to you, in your marriage area of the house.

To enhance an already fantastic relationship, you can strengthen the marriage areas of the land, home and bedroom. Cure any weakness, so they will not get into your relationship chi. Add live lush plants in the bedroom to keep a relationship fresh and alive, nine is best.

If a relationship is challenged, check to see if you have opposing zodiac signs. See pages 133-135. Check for arguing doors in the home, particularly in the marriage/partnership gua of the house and anywhere in or around the master bedroom. Cure any piercing arrows that are facing to shooting chi at the bed. Cure a mandarin duck stairway in any area of the home. Cure detached buildings in the partnership area of the home. We have hundreds of factors to review.

Career

The front door has a special impact on your career regardless if it is in Knowledge/Wisdom, Career or Helpful People/Friends. Career is your day to day activities, so if you are retired, semi-retired or serve your community in a volunteer capacity, this energy reflection shows up here   . It is your path and how your life flows. Like the waters of the earth, it moves.

Whether you are creating a new career, enhancing or ensuring security in one, Feng Shui can be most beneficial. If you wish to move your career along, place a fan or some type of object that moves. If you are looking for expansion or recognition, you may consider hanging a large clear beautiful mirror. Adding a powerful object (symbolic or otherwise) in-between your mattress and bed may be the most enhancing way to activate the energy of your career. Use clear heartfelt intention with the Three Secrets to get the most effect. Don't forget how influential your stove has on your career.

Children

This area is for the joy of your life, your offspring and just plain fun. There are very powerful mystical cures to help in conception. I have seen some beautiful results. The only time it seemed to not work in a timely fashion, my client and I then realized if she had the child when she most wanted, it would have been an opposing zodiac animal to her, creating conflict and lessons throughout their lives. She had the child in the very next year that it was beneficial and not confrontational. See the last section in this chapter on the Chinese Zodiac energy.

If you are not having enough fun in life, need more creative energy or want to conceive a child, enhance your children areas of your land, home and bedroom. The element is metal. If appropriate place metal in all three of these areas. White is the color, however be mindful of white flowers too close to the house in any Bagua area including Children. This has a negative mystical effect and I have seen it be accurate many times.

You can also place cures of Kuan Yin, the Goddess of Mercy & Compassion who is the most powerful benefactor for women and children. Using art or pictures of a literal connection to children or babies may be another choice. Be mindful of the specific meaning of the art to you. Be clear and precise when making your intentions.

Helpful People

This is a very special place for me. Helpful people relates to travel, heavenly energies, the father/brother, mostly giving back to the universe, people who you help and those who help you.
If you enjoy travel, place items that are about the place you wish to travel to in the helpful people area of your home or

bedroom. I have been known to place my passport in-between the mattress and box spring of the helpful people area
of my bed. Last year, I was given the opportunity to fly to
Germany and speak on Feng Shui aboard the Queen Mary. It
was quite an adventure. It came out of the blue, or through
the magic of Feng Shui.

In the time period, many real estate markets are correcting,
or tougher than they have been in the past. This area, the
helpful people area can be beneficial when working with the
energy to help people to find the best property to buy and to
help those sell. If you need movement, place a moving object. Windchimes are also a great way to activate this energy.

Helpful people can help people who have financial
challenges as well. When you give from the heart of your
time, energy, love, things and even money, it opens up
energy to receive. Do acts of giving and make sure that any
weaknesses are corrected in helpful people, so you can enjoy
prosperity and balance.

Fame/Reputation

Few people really need their name in the limelight. (I may
be wrong on this, as the contest tv shows seems to be all the
rage) However, this area is for someone who needs to be
known, well known. Politicians, celebrities, and businesses
that need to maintain or build reputation. The energy is
fire and the color is red. Sound can be very beneficial here
as well.

The part about this area that I love, is the deeper meanings of
fame. It is a connection to your soul, finding your authentic
passion, what really will bring out your best and help you to
live your truth. When someone wants a new career or path

in life, I have used the energies that create a profound connection in Feng Shui. They are Career (the path, journey, your walk), Fame (your talk, inspiration to soul) and Children (your joy – fun, creative energy, and child like innocence and wonderment). When you place cures in these areas with the intention to create a new path, amazing things happen.

Family

Family connections are important, even if they cannot be done with the original biological family for whatever reason. Cure any missing piece, weakness or imbalance. Build the energy for harmony and fulfillment. If harmony or balance is needed, you may consider using cures that relate to the five elements.

Grandmaster Lin Yun has created a global community. He is father figure and real godfather to so many people that I am not sure it can be counted. The community of us who go to workshops each year have become an extended family. Our only connection is His Holiness Grandmaster Lin Yun. It is a wonderful experience and the relationships and love is very special to so many of us.

Knowledge/Spirituality

There is so much to learn. Being open and teachable is something that was instilled in me as a child. I am grateful for that. Curiosity and knowing there was more was a driving force as well. When people are working on degrees or working on figuring out a new solution this is the space to work on that chi. Mirrors are great cures in this location. The mystical sun moon mirror is a fabulous tool to open up your wisdom eye.

Knowledge is not only what you know but how well you use what you do know. The trigram is the mountain. Placing a beautiful piece of art that shows a magnificent or a series of mountains may be beneficial here. Powered objects can also be of great use in this location.

Make sure that you cure any imbalance on the land, in the home, in the study area, in the bedroom, in the office and in the kitchen when it comes to creating positive energy with knowledge. Do cures in three locations. You can also use the energy of the bed.

Chinese Zodiac Energies

Yearly Zodiac enhancements are powerful cures for your overall energy. It is auspicious and powerful to carry a charm, a jade or jade like charm, a three dimensional object the partner of the zodiac animal of the year, it can create beneficial energy for you.

Beginning 2/18/07 the Year of the Boar, it is auspicious to carry a tiger with you for when the Tiger and the Boar are together the chi is high and good things happen. It is said that this compatible energy can avert disaster, bring many blessings and attract wealth. You can wear a tiger on a necklace, bracelet, or a pin, be creative. You can tie one to your key chain, place in your wallet or purse. The technical application is not as important as just doing it. February 8, 2008 will be the year of the earth Rat. The Ox is the most compatible with the Rat. Wear a jade Ox charm from 2/8/08 to 1/26/09 for auspicious energy

Most Compatibles
  • Rat – Ox

- Tiger – Boar
- Rabbit – Dog
- Dragon – Rooster
- Snake – Monkey
- Horse – Sheep

Zodiac Animals are determined by year, the lunar year. Each year the first day of the year changes, as it is determined by the lunar month. So, if your birthday is in January or February it may actually be the zodiac animal of the previous year. The animals change every year, there are 12 animals.

This is the order: Rat, Ox, Tiger, Rabbit, Dragon, Snake, Horse, Sheep, Monkey, Rooster, Dog, and Pig.

- Rat years are 1936, 1948, 1960, 1972, 1984, 1996.

- Ox years are 1937, 1949, 1961, 1973, 1985, 1997.

- Tiger years are 1938, 1950, 1962, 1974, 1986, 1998.

- Rabbit years are 1939, 1951, 1963, 1975, 1987, 1999.

- Dragon years are 1940, 1952, 1964, 1976, 1988, 2000.

- Snake years are 1941, 1953, 1965, 1977, 1989, 2001.

- Horse years are 1942, 1954, 1966, 1978, 1990, 2002.

- Sheep years are 1943, 1955, 1967, 1979, 1991, 2003.

- Monkey years are 1944, 1956, 1968, 1980, 1992, 2004.

- Rooster years are 1945, 1957, 1969, 1981, 1993, 2005.

• Dog years are 1946, 1958, 1970, 1982, 1994, 2006.

• Pig/Boar years are 1947, 1959, 1971,1983, 1995, 2007.

There are other Positive Relationships called the Three Harmonies and these are:

          Rat—- Monkey—- Dragon
          Ox—- Snake—- Rooster
          Tiger —- Horse—- Dog
          Rabbit —- Sheep—- Pig/Boar

There are the most confrontational relationships as well, which Professor has given us a secret method to offset the opposition that may ensue when there are the pairing of zodiac relations listed below.

      • Rat – Sheep
      • Ox - Horse
      • Tiger – Snake
      • Rabbit – Dragon
      • Monkey – Pig/Boar

Chapter 12
What to do first? Levels of Feng Shui

K eeping it simple, have fun when you Feng Shui your home!

I started teaching and consulting on Feng Shui in 1995, I love it and really like to help people with their spaces, real estate and lives. Many people have commented on how 'user' friendly I have been able to convey its basic principles. You can go to very many levels, yet to begin keep it simple.

Overlay the Bagua on your home, its land and most importantly your bedroom. Cure any missing pieces. (It is not necessary and can be quite overwhelming to try and place the Bagua on each and every room in your home. The point becomes moot.)

When you want to shift the energy, make an enhancement or activate a special part of your life, do it on 3 levels. If you want to enhance wealth, adjust the wealth on your land, home and bedroom. You can adjust your bed instead of the land or home, if you wish.

Really work with the energy of your front door. Since this is the space that all the positive energy you attract will enter your home it is very important.

The 3 main areas of chi in your home are the front door, your bedroom and the kitchen. If you need to fix or perhaps to buy a new front door, bed or stove, make it a priority.

Go about making your energy adjustments with joy. Do not stress over it, simply do it. Go with the flow.

If you have true clutter, address it. (Look to pages 115-119 on clutter). Know that there is a reason for its existence and if you do not address that while you are clearing and organizing, it will return. Sometimes, clutter that stems from a deep psychological issue, should be dealt with slowly, not quick which can be too harsh.

General maintenance helps to keep the chi high and pleasant in your home. Leaks of water can cause health conditions. Home maintenance is a constant responsibility. Some things will need to be fixed asap, others can be scheduled in the near future.

Before you do adjustments to activate an area fix all you can and make sure the space is nice and clean. Clean your home before a space clearing and before New Years in the calendar year and especially in the Chinese New Year. Let go of the old and make a clear clean path for the new chi to be placed in your life and home.

140

Appendix One
Information

Information for you to obtain

Below is a list of the many types of information and services that are available through Kathy Mann and website, *www.fengshui108.com, sales@fengshui108.com* . All of the below information is deeper knowledge and methods and will require an exchange of the red envelopes. Please email us for details on the topic or service you need.

Overlay of the Bagua on your home, land, or workspace

> Health Index - a to z complete
> One diagnosis or condition at a time.
>
> World of Wealth Cures
> - Nine
> - 27
> - 81
> - 99
> - 108
> - All
>
> Stove Details, Cures and Information
>
> Front Door – all you would need to know
>
> Career Enhancements
> - New Positions
> - Security
> - Salary
> - Recognition
>
> Relationship/Marriage/Love/Partnership
> - Manifesting a new relationship
> - Strengthening an existing relationship
> - Cures to help a troubled relationship

Practitioner Training Manual
- Part I
- Part II•
- Part III is an on-site teaching (dvd may be available in the future)
- Advanced Teachings - topics include 5 elements, secret methods, unusual cures and more…
- Meditations

Landscape Details, Design and Methods of Enhancing the Chi

Chi Adjustments
- Core Teachings
- The Complete Index

What to look for when buying a home

Complete Real Estate Manual

How to sell your home with Feng Shui

Website tips

Cures for specific events:
- to change luck to good
- Litigation
- Marriage
- Conception
- Admission to School
- Promotion
- Finding a Mate

Cures to use in conjunction with the principles of the movie 'The Secret'

Commercial Feng Shui

- Office (general and specific)
- Retail
- Manufacturing
- Restaurants
- Development, community and urban planning
- Health Care Facilities
- Logo Design
- Spa
- Health Club
- Color Choices

Appendix Two
Case Studies

Interesting Actual Case Studies

My client decided to take some suggestions from a class she came to. She cleared away a room of boxes that was in a majority of her wealth area. Soon afterward, she received an unexpected raise, and a gift from a distant relative.

During the first year I was doing Feng Shui, a friend who is a single mother who is self-employed, needed money in a big way. I was still working in corporate America. She called me at work. I asked her to honor the red envelope ritual with three red envelopes, she did. I gave her a ritual to bring money to her. She did the cure it was 12:20pm. She called me at 1:10 and her ex-husband came to her door with money, and the mortgage broker gave her a home equity loan when no one else would. We both had chills. She came by my house that night and gave me the red envelopes to empower the continued energy.

House Sales. I have so many success stories. One in 2004 where my realtor client had a contract that closed in 9 days 10 minutes after I did the chi adjustment. This was a rare situation. It was her home and she had too much emotional pain connected to the house. The investor did work on the house and asked her to list it a month later.

One gentleman wanted the home to not be torn down. He wanted full value for the house in a very quick way. he investor who bought her house, did cosmetic work on it, then requested that she list it and she then sold it in weeks.

Another client worked with me long distance, she was in Australia. We talked over the phone, and after the home was on the market for 8 months, she received 2 offers in the next few weeks and the second offer was the winner.

New business. My clients painted the building a beautiful shade of purple. Business was so good they had to hire more people right away.

Restaurant - business was slow. My clients took over a location that had numerous restaurant failures. I did a powerful chi adjustment. They ran out of food off and on for the next two weeks until the growth leveled to a constant. Great success, great happiness.

Recommended Authentic Black Sect Authors:

• Grand Master Lin Yun, Sara Rossbach

• David Daniel Kennedy, Steven Post

• Nancy Santopietro, Juan Alvarez,

There are numerous books that are only in Chinese, if you prefer these authors please contact *www.yunlintemple.org* for references.

Appendix Three
Kathy Mann's full background

Kathy Mann's full background

Kathy Mann, Abundant Feng Shui Creations

Kathy Mann is the founder and owner of the successful *Abundant Feng Shui Creations* business headquartered in Tampa, Florida. Kathy built this enlightened company with her more than 14 years of experience in delivering powerful professional and personalized Feng Shui consulting and education.

Kathy's extensive background assures that her clients receive the most in-depth benefits offered through extensive Feng Shui practices. She is the most qualified and authoritative Feng Shui professional in the Tampa Bay area, exclusively in the Black Sect Tradition of Feng Shui. Her skillful guidance makes a long-lasting impression on her numerous clients. In fact, more than 65% of Kathy's clients return for more expanded assistance.

To strengthen her art, Kathy traveled extensively in the United States and China to acquire her considerable expertise. She has learned much at the valuable hands of His Holiness Grandmaster Lin Yun. He is the founder and supreme leader of Black Sect Tantric Buddhism Feng Shui. Kathy attended more than 40 classes with the Grandmaster and mentored with his senior students. In total, her collective study hours exceed 3,000 in class and on-site studies.

As proof of the Grandmaster's confidence in her abilities, Kathy was granted permission to use the Black Sect Tantric name in her training programs. She also coordinated his 2003 teaching visit to Tampa Bay.

Services offered through *Abundant Feng Shui Creations* include:

- Commercial assessments and design for optimum results.
- Real estate consulting for quick smooth transactions.
- Residential assessments and design for harmony and quality of life.
- Site location selection consultations for homes and businesses.
- Chi adjustments, Space Clearings, Blessing & Grand Opening Ceremonies.
- Speaking programs for community and business groups.
- Classes, Workshops & Seminars – ranging from Home Design, Landscape Design, Wealth Enhancing, Commercial Design, Health, Color… to a full program for Feng Shui Practitioners.
- Coaching and training for practitioners.
- Presented three programs to the passenger on the Queen Mary August 2006
- October 2006, Kathy conducted 2 programs for guests at Canyon Ranch Spa in Tucson, AZ and one program for the employees.

Kathy's knowledge and expertise is highly sought after by practitioners and the public. Her international work experience exceeds 3,500 consultations helping clients in homes and businesses.

Her work and advice on Feng Shui are published throughout the United States, Hong Kong and China. Examples of her widespread influence include:

- Published in the *Feng Shui Anthology*, a book edited by Jamie Lin.
- Published in *Sell your Home Faster with Feng Shui*, a book written by Holly Ziegler.
- Published numerous articles on the Internet, spanning the globe.

Writes her own monthly Feng Shui newsletter since 1999.

Created Feng Shui correspondence courses in basic to advanced teachings.
Produced a professionally recorded lecture on Feng Shui principles, distributed internationally.

Been interviewed by local Florida TV stations and a national program for educational television, completed 11 programs for community access TV and spotlighted in local newspapers.

Received publication in national periodicals to include *Unique Homes, Design Digest, Working Mother* and *Spirit Airlines.*

Her long-held knowledge has ignited her passion of enlightening others about the numerous benefits of Feng Shui. Kathy has taught more than 380 classes.

Not only that, but Kathy has designed 45 classes including a professional training program, advanced level classes, an apprentice program, basic program and many specific topics on all level classes. She is often considered the Expert's Expert.

From a professional perspective, Kathy has a strong sense of ethics and integrity in her relationships. Her work style is described as results oriented. She is known for her down-to-earth style in relaying information to clients and students without losing the integrity of the work. Kathy is recognized for her fast processing of space details that affords a quick, proficient analysis for clients.

Kathy does not believe in cookie-cutter answers to the ancient art of placement. She provides customized environmental programs designed to reflect the occupant's energy and sense of style. She creates corporate and home dwellings that place the highest standards of living for the mind, body and spirit.

She also has a wealth of experience in the field of real estate. Her success paved the way for her to receive a Florida Real Estate License in 2000. She is actively representing clients working with Stipe Realty Group, LLC in south Tampa. Kathy's work is made stronger by her previous career in business consulting and marketing. She earned a Bachelor of Science in Business from the University of Central Florida in 1982.

With Kathy Mann steadily at its helm, *Abundant Feng Shui Creations'* vision is to facilitate the art and science of energizing and harmonizing home and work environments for prosperity and vitality. Her mission is to provide life transformational changes and improvements in all aspects of life and work for her clients.

Kathy Mann
Abundant Feng Shui Creations
P.O. Box 20683
Tampa, FL 33622
Telephone: (888) 339-9927
Web site: *www.fengshui108.com*
Email: *consulting@fengshui108.com*

識得道中道　方悟禪外禪

二〇〇七年丁亥端午礫書持咒以為

Kathy MANN CH'S, FENGSHUI and YOU 大著讀者　作者編者園府新福增慧祿圭

奄宗黑敖曇林禪寺

寺禪林曇時客庚見立

紫虹軒

Center calligraphy: ZEN

Inscription from right:

"Only when one learns the Tao within the Tao,
Could one be enlightened of the Zen beyond the Zen."

Written with cinnabar while chanting mantras on the Dragon
Boat Festival, the Fifth Day of the Fifth Lunar Month, 2007.
This calligraphy bestows blessings upon the entire household of
the author, editor, and readers, and prays that they receive auspicious luck, increased wisdom, and safety.

Composed by Lin Yun of Black Sect Tantric Buddhism Yun Lin
Temple, while a visitor at the study of disciple Crystal Chu.

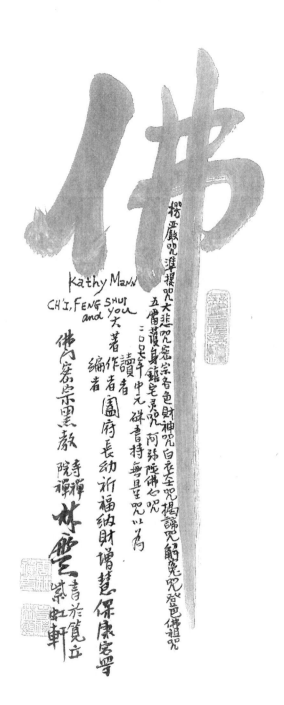

佛

楞嚴咒 准提咒 大悲咒 慈宗 各色財神咒 白衣大士咒 揭諦咒 解冤咒 啟巴佛道咒
五層護身 鎮宅靈咒 兩歸依佛心咒
二〇〇年中元 碟書持 無量咒以為

Kathy Mann

CH'I, FENG and SHUI YOU

大 著

讀者

作者 園府長幼 祈福納財 譜慧 保康宅寧

編者

佛門寮宗黑教 寺禪 院禪 林豐 書於覓立 紫虹軒

Center calligraphy: BUDDHA
Inscription from right:

The Surangama Mantra, the Chandi Boddhisatva Mantra, the
Great Compassion Mantra, the Tantric Buddhist Various – col-
ored Deities of Wealth Mantras, The White-robed Kuan-Yin
Mantra, the Heart Calming Mantra, the Medicine Buddha
Mantra, the Lord Tonpa Sherab Mantra, the Five Thunder
Protectors Mantra, the Amitabba Mantra.

Written in cinnabar while chanting infinite numbers of mantras
on the Ghost Festival, the 15th day of the Seventh Lunar Month,
2007. This calligraphy bestows Blessings upon the entire household of the author, editor, and readers of this new book, and prays
that they will have auspicious luck, plentiful wealth, increased
wisdom, and peaceful safety.

Composed by Lin Yun of Black Sect Tantric Buddhism Yun Lin
Temple, while a visitor at the study of disciple Crystal Chu.

Printed in the United States
124232LV00001BD/154-201/P